WHERE HAS MUM GONE

A MEMOIR OF GROWING UP WITH MY MOTHER'S

MENTAL ILLNESS

This edition 2024

Copyright © Gregory Kinchin 2024

All rights reserved.
No part of this book may be reproduced, stored in a retrieval system or transmitted, in any form or by any means, electronic, mechanical, photocopying, recording or otherwise, or used in any manner without written permission of the copyright owner except for the use of quotations in a book review.

First paperback edition March 2024

pub@itchikinch.com

ISBN: 9798878870993

WHERE HAS MUM GONE

A MEMOIR OF GROWING UP WITH MY MOTHER'S MENTAL ILLNESS

GREGORY KINCHIN

CHAPTER 1

THE FIRST TIME

I was about eight and we were told we had the choice of having a TV, or a piano. Or should I say we were told we might get a TV or a piano. Thank goodness we got both in the end. Only one person could play the piano!

The back room was the dining room of our three-bedroom semi, and this is where the piano eventually lived. My sister had followed music at school, was showing ability and needed a piano at home to practice. But this was not the only source of music in the house. There was also a radiogram, which I barely remember getting used, except for the radio occasionally. It was clear that my parents weren't about to buy more than a couple of records to play on it . . . ever. And the ones we had were from the first days it had been bought, in the excitement of the moment. Mantovani was one to give you a flavour of the time and interest in the new market of pop and modern music. We're talking mid- 60′s. Rock n Roll and the early Beatles were a little after my middle ageing parents and, as I say, I was only about eight.

The room also contained a sideboard with bowls of fruit and several piles of envelopes and paper. On the wall above was fixed a letter rack. This was stuffed with envelopes which never seemed to change. But in addition, 'the cane' was also stuffed in that rack. A length of bamboo that had great threatening power if we behaved badly and my mother was at the end of her tether. That didn't seem such an uncommon state. If 'wait till your father gets home' didn't work, the threat and wave of the cane just might! I don't think I was ever on a colliding course with it, so I guess it must've worked . . . mostly. Perhaps a good dodger. In my child's mind's eye that cane was at least three feet long, but in truth it was only about eighteen inches at best. My mum was raising three children aged eight to sixteen. The cane was her last line of defence.

Dad was at work. I remember this one day, I climbed onto the old three-seater sofa where mum was sitting. Sometimes, I would sit and nudge up next to her, put my face cheek to cheek with hers, and without turning my head, look sideways and tell her to look at me too. That strange look would make her laugh. I would do it often as my way of asking for that little bit of love and attention. The sofa was a very old and worn utility one with torn stringy bits, especially at the floor edge. I remember knowing that she was a bit grumpy but didn't think her mood would apply to me. I was the youngest of the three of us, you see, and usually conflict, which sometimes used to fly around, didn't come as far as me because of that. I had an age dispensation, so to speak. I lay on the other cushions to rest my head on mum's lap. Rather than acceptance, her words were short, abrupt and cold. She didn't want me there. I felt that sudden coldness in her tone to me. It upset me, which I guess was to be expected. But I wasn't just being pushed away.

Of course, these things happen to any child, and before long, some reassurance and love would come and make everything better again. But she was irritated by something elsewhere. It made me feel vulnerable and hurt. So much so that I wouldn't visit that place again unless I was invited. Any warmth had gone and as a young boy, I felt the rejection.

This was an event that stayed with me. Mum had become absorbed into her own mind.

A door was closing to me.
And I felt that difference.

CHAPTER 2

SERENDIPITY

The Dartington Literary Festival is an event I would probably never have thought of going to myself, as I am not, and never have been, an avid book reader. I wish I could have been. My father didn't read, but my mother was a good reader when she was younger, she told me, and she picked that up from seeing her father always with his nose in a book. There was a time, before my teens, when she would try and get me to read; threatening me with having to stay home till I did. But the idea wasn't pursued with a tone that could persuade me. It wasn't sold with any appeal. I was also a little sensitive and needed a more loving cajoling approach, a style not commonly used in our house. Besides, there was too much else going on for me to be settled enough to clear my mind and get engrossed in a book.

So, how did I come to be considering attending at the Dartington Literary Festival?

It started with the fact that though I am sixty-six, divorced thirteen years, I found myself on a dating site. I had been exploring the site when a lovely lady popped up on my computer. This was the only time in my experience first messages overlapped. Well, this is a good omen, I thought. She looked lovely in her photos and her profile was individual, interesting, colourful, and lively. Everything was there to trigger my imagination.

We struck up a conversation. In the opening exchange I asked, 'what you are doing being so far away?' She was just outside Leeds in Yorkshire, and I was southwest of London in Surrey. Distance had always been an issue for me; how do you do anything on a whim when you're 200 miles away?

'I am planning to retire to the southwest,' she replied and named some towns she had already researched. Not entirely a solution to my concerns, but enough to throw everything up in the air for now and go with the flow of the moment. This allowed me the excuse to continue with the conversation. As I say, I was not an avid reader, but this lady was, and a reader with a passion.

As the conversation grew, It turned out that this lady had visited Dartington Literary Festival for many years and was about to visit for the 2022 season. At this point, I only knew her as Tigger, her profile name. And as her profile said, 'the most wonderful thing about Tigger is, I'm the only one!'

Out of curiosity, I looked at the festival website and scrolled through all the events. I surprised myself by being able to find lots of interesting talks. My first thought was that I should also like to go to the festival.

But that idea was fraught with difficulties. A first meet at an established event with Tigger. She would be with many friends, who she had met over the years. She planned to chat and exchange ideas, maybe have lunch and drinks. The idea of showing up sounded fun but would've been unfair to suggest. I retreated from that idea reluctantly.

I noticed one of the talks by a writer called Anna Wilson. She had written a book called *A Place for Everything, My Mother Autism and Me*. I read her introduction online and for some reason immediately imagined myself there at the session, wanting to stand up and ask a question. It was a surprisingly immediate reaction but I felt I could see a common pattern in our experiences. We had both lived through family events that would go on to influence our lives, probably in very different ways and likely changed us. I could relate to that and wanted to find out how she had experienced living with her mother and how she comprehended the consequences. It wasn't something I was looking for, but her words touched me, and I wanted to find out more. I wanted to ask one question in particular.

'You knew things were different. I knew things were different, though I didn't know how or why. But I realised when I got older what the differences were and, eventually, what they meant. Can you relate to that?'

The thought of this question filled me with emotion and stayed with me a while. I'd ignited my own emotions.

I left my computer, took a breather and walked down the road to the supermarket. As I walked that emotion I felt was still brimming right near the surface. I walked down the aisles of half the shop before I could get past it and concentrate. I hadn't realised those emotions were so close to the surface and could be charged so easily.

A sensitive reaction you might think, and I would not normally consider myself over emotional, but sometimes things grab me. Things I relate strongly to, and the perceived connection here to my own experience was one of those moments I couldn't let go. It took me back to points I will write in my story where finding someone who had similar experiences was nigh impossible. And when you do, the moment can feel life changing. To find someone whose experiences might have been on a par with your own can feel like a life saver, because you can share and identify with them.

That is the big reason I am writing this story. All our stories are unique, but somebody out there may be hearing this for the first time, and feeling their experience is shared can be so valuable when you might otherwise feel isolated.

I have not read Anna Wilson's book and will not until I have finished writing this. I suspect it will be a very different story to mine. Nevertheless, it was a trigger for me. What this encounter made me realise was that if Anna Wilson had found her very valuable life experience could create great educational value to others in a book, then there could be great value for someone in laying out my experiences too, because shared recognisable experiences can be so valuable to others who have had life disruption. I felt that the moment you can put a name to a condition or recognise a behaviour can give extraordinary relief and understanding. A lifeline. Not necessarily a diagnosis, partly because the diagnosis of mental health conditions can be a long time coming, and sometimes longer than that. And even then, a professional diagnosis can tell you what's happening at that given time but may well not consider the many years of managing and suffering which got you to that moment. Treatment of course can only be based on the here and now. Something we found to be a frustrating reality, but really an obvious fact.

So thank you Tigger for the trigger. Even if we never meet, I love you already x

I am, in fact, away on holiday writing this. I have time on my hands and space in my head, a sea view to get lost in, helped by a few shots of caffeine and even a little alcohol to help me calmly consider my thoughts. I realise that Tigger will be fully ensconced in the festival and reuniting with all her wonderful friends and minds she has related with over recent years. She described it as 'like a university for grown-ups in a beautiful setting'.

Over the next two weeks I will have spent many hours writing this book. The festival will be over, I will be home and maybe I will be able to meet Tigger around Bristol on her way home, as we have established that both our younger children live in the city.

    Oh how the world has changed.

    And oh. What an amazing coincidence!

CHAPTER 3

IDENTIFICATION

Nothing is simple for family or sufferer, spouse, or sibling when you come to living with a parent with a type of schizophrenia. All are dramatically affected, lives changed and never to be resolved, but managed somehow in whichever way possible. Often the illnesses not identified, recognised, or treated.

I was born in 1957, and mental illness was little understood, a taboo subject in the mid-1960s when my story begins, other than locking people away. Families had to cope with situations they did not understand. There were many cases where any type of diagnosis was never achieved, if they were recognised at all. If recognised, then probably not treated. If treated, then probably only because behaviours were such that they could not be ignored, because they were a danger to life.

It is thought that around 10% of people with schizophrenia will die by their own hand within ten years of diagnosis and a further 15% will attempt suicide unsuccessfully.

Living with schizophrenia

That's 25% already, and 10% within ten years of diagnosis begs the question of the unknown figure of those who take their own lives without diagnosis. An impossible number to calculate. But cannot be ignored.

For us, there were two periods in my mother's life, quite far apart, when we thought we might lose her. In simple terms, my mum most likely suffered from Paranoid Schizophrenia. Nowadays, there might be all sorts of other symptoms identified whether that be post-natal depression, menopausal depression, or many other conditions, because that is how the recognition of mental illnesses has progressed and is understood. As with causes of depression, from what I have seen, many diagnoses can either change or develop frequently, demonstrating just how difficult and complex it is to simply identify mental illness.

This brings us to the question – What is schizophrenia?

Schizophrenia is a mental illness which affects the way you think.
The symptoms may affect how you cope with day-to-day life.
You could be diagnosed with schizophrenia if you experience some of the following symptoms.

- *Hallucinations*
- *Delusions*
- *Disorganised thinking*
- *Lack of motivation*
- *Slow movement*
- *Change in sleep patterns*
- *Poor grooming or hygiene*
- *Changes in body language and emotions*
- *Less interest in social activities*
- *Low sex drive*

Everyone's experience of schizophrenia is different. Not everyone with schizophrenia will experience all these symptoms.

Living with schizophrenia

Treatment often meant being sent to institutions to separate unconventional behaviours from 'normal' society. I lived near Epsom in Surrey which had more than the average number of these institutions, thankfully since demolished.

Behind closed doors at home was an entirely different matter. 'She's had a mental breakdown' was a common way to explain some absent or non-conforming behaviour, in a kind of 'respectable' way. Somewhere to put the problem, but also sometimes the only way to excuse a mentally ill person when you feel sure others wouldn't understand.

And so, even in our modern world, when I found myself reacting to someone telling a story I might relate to, it is clear that identifying and sharing first hand experiences can potentially be such a comfort and help to us all. I often say in the relating of my story that I don't remember exactly when or where an event took place. On occasion I could've perhaps asked around and acquired some more detail. This isn't careless work on my part, it is a part of the story, and an important one for me. In fact in reading other people's accounts, I've noticed it is not uncommon for this detail to be difficult to pin down. Of course, my story must make sense, but this story is one of my mother, her fight with her world and my experience of my mother as I grew up. It is a journey of extreme emotion, strength and survival for her. These are the things which ultimately drove her extraordinary ninety-seven years of life, with all the tension turmoil and torment that involved.

The main part of my story, my mother, has completed, and that is the story I wish to share with you. I will always carry the effect it has had on me as we all do with our life stories and choices, but my desire is that somebody reading this may be able to identify and relate to some or many of those experiences, hopefully communicating something they find some comfort or understanding in. That, for me, is where I hope there is value.

CHAPTER 4

MUM'S ROOTS

Both my parents grew up in the East End in the Millwall area. My mother was slightly better off, as her father was a docker and had a permanent job. Having three brothers, two particularly boisterous, and being the only girl, she was unsurprisingly close to her mother. I never met my grandmother as although I believe she lived till she was seventy, she had passed before I came along. My memory is only of mum's father and how she felt about him. Mum had a birth mark on her face which in her younger years made her self conscious.

She would recall how two of her three brothers would come home from the local pub, swinging on the doors drunk and piss in a pot on the landing. Outside toilets of course were standard. These, and more, were memories unsurprisingly she never held with any joy. Her eldest brother was kindest to her, not as boisterous as the other two. He would come home from work and teach her what he had learned in his job to help her get on. He was a much gentler man than his two younger brothers.

Her dad was an avid reader, and that was where mum got her habit from. He always had a book on the go. It seemed almost contradictory given his forthright character which mum didn't seem to easily deal with. By her account he was a bully and cruel to her. She used to tell us how he would smack her hand away if she put it near her face. When I was very young, we would visit and my memory is of a rough character who I didn't much warm to as a young shy and sensitive boy. He was white haired and red skinned, usually unshaven. Probably because he had bad skin which looked dry and eczema like. Even from that young age I still have that picture in my mind of him. What became apparent some years later was that my mother had grown to hate him. This became evident when she later received a telephone call to inform her of his death. Mum never received telephone calls, she had no reason to at the time. I listened in the front room whilst she took the call in the hall. It was clearly an important call. There was a hint of emotion at first as she was given the news. She came back into the lounge and sat down. After her initial reaction, a hardness came over her. Of course, she was upset at losing her father, even though they had little or no contact now.

But it was already in her mind.

She wasn't going to shed a tear for him.

What I wouldn't have realised from that young age, well before I was a teenager, was the stage was already being set for the tragedy that was to follow.

Living in Surrey far away from the East End, visits were infrequent, and those made were always surprise visits met with 'why didn't you say you were coming?' I never understood why we would always visit in that way. It was as if it would minimise the impact of the visit. To plan it would be too definite. A drop in and drop out idea was always the way with all our relatives. If we were lucky there would be a tin of salmon in the cupboard we could have for some tea. That was posh.

My dad often said mum was the brighter of them both, and that she didn't make friends easily. But not long before

mum and dad got married, she contracted meningitis. An illness which was as dangerous then as it is now, and her dose of it was no exception. She spent several days in a coma but recovered with no known complications.
Looking back, mum had a challenging upbringing. She had lived through the Second World War, was bombed out of one home whilst in a shelter and survived a serious life-threatening illness. Her confidence was knocked by her father's behaviour and having a facial birthmark. It is hard not to imagine that these factors may have played a critical part in her future mental health.

Nobody knows exactly what causes schizophrenia; it is likely to be the result of several factors.

For example:

• Stress. Some people can develop the illness as a result of a stressful event, such as the death of a loved one or the loss of a job.

- *Genetics. You are more likely to develop schizophrenia if you have a close relation with the illness.*
- *Brain damage. This is usually damage that has stopped your brain from growing normally when your mother was pregnant. Or during birth.*
- *Drugs and alcohol. Research has shown that stronger forms of cannabis increase your risk of developing schizophrenia.*
- *A difficult childhood. If you were deprived, or abused, as a child this can increase your risk of developing a mental illness. Including schizophrenia.*

There is research to suggest that there may be an association between menopause and schizophrenia. This may be due to the hormonal change during this stage of life

for women

Rethink Mental Illness

CHAPTER 5

DAD'S ROOTS

My dad came from a family of eight children, one older brother and six sisters His childhood complied more to the stereotypical East Ender life, where families were a unit and got on with neighbours, helping each other out. He was second from youngest, and with five older sisters and one younger. I think fair to say he was a little spoilt. The eldest sister very much played the role of parent too. His mother apparently had thirty-two pregnancies, sixteen births, only the eight of which survived.

His mother was also the local midwife and laid out the dead. It is no wonder eldest daughter played mum! Though often sleeping under the stairs, which he never complained about when reminiscing, I think my dad was content, well looked after and well fed. He'd talk about pulling driftwood out from the Thames and getting a 'hap'orth' (or whatever it was) of leftover batter bits from the fish n chip shop fryer. He always enjoyed his 'grub' as he often referred to it as. To help ends meet, they took in a lodger to what was a three-bedroom terraced house in Havana Street. This is why he used to sleep on the sofa or under the stairs. One bedroom for his parents, one for the six girls, and the last for the lodger. The kitchen was off limits when the girls would be having their bath time in the tub. Even peeping through the window!

Mum and dad grew up locally and went to the same school. They would often walk the tunnel under the Thames to Greenwich in their courting years. In photos of them from this period, they would appear to be happy and content. They were childhood sweethearts after all and having escorted his sweetheart home dad could often be heard whistling away as he made his way home.
But there were many fallings out between siblings, which mum didn't deal well with.

During the war, after the help that her eldest brother had given her, mum worked in the War Office, and dad was in the RAF as groundcrew. When they were twenty-one in 1941, he got home leave so they could get married. I think he had already lost a lot of his hair at this point. He wouldn't have an injection at the dentist, but the scare of an appendix operation put the wind up him as they used to say, and had its consequences.

CHAPTER 6

FAMILY

My brother was born within the sound of Bow bells in 1949, my mother was twenty-eight. My sister was not to be born until 1954, but at some point, my mother decided she wanted to move away from the East End to make a better life for her family. An address, where you lived in those days was important if you wanted to get on. My dad had gone back to the advertising company in Soho, where he worked as tea boy before the war. He worked hard and eventually made his way up to being a director before retiring.

Shortly before I was born, they moved to Tolworth in Surrey. House prices were too high to buy, even though my dad had a reasonable job in London. So renting was the only option. My mother was a worrier, and was always concerned about dad's job, and looking after it. You couldn't blow up a paper bag and bang it cos you'd 'bust your father out of work', she use to say!

They had an option to buy the house they were renting, but it was too much money, and eventually they moved to a similar slightly smaller rented house in Tolworth. My mother was religious, which was to prove both good and bad in her experiences. The move worked out well for her since the local Catholic Church was at the end of our road. Dad was between an agnostic and an atheist. Religion didn't interest him. Although an intelligent woman, my mother unsurprisingly had some naiveties. The adjustment to a different life in Surrey from the East End I believe was harder than she imagined. Her desire to put the London Docklands behind her outweighed the complexity of moving to a different area, a different way of living. Making friends was difficult for my mother, and the anxiety of raising three children, learning new ways and trying to fit in made making friends a huge hurdle. My father often worked late and returned home tired and found it hard to deal with problems at home. Hard

I think to look after my mum who needed his reassurance and support. And I suspect she was unaware of what his needs might have been too. All might normally be cushioned with family nearby or local friends. But those avenues of support were now out of reach or non-existent. These beginnings of isolation were to replicate in my experiences and have profound consequences for me as I was growing up.

One of my earliest memories was me slipping away one day with a few pennies to the sweet shop on the corner, wondering if I could get back with a Milky Way before I was missed. An achievement, as mum was such a worrier and usually very alert because of that. Wherever did I get that money from? But I knew where the Milky Ways were.

Mondays were washing day. The kitchen and the twin tub would seem to be going all day. That is, when we got a twin tub. Before it was much harder work. Getting a twin tub was a bit like eating an ice cream and having a foot rub at the same time by comparison. Modern technology was arriving, though still very hard work. We still used the larder and had no fridge. Mum's sleeves would be rolled up and she would complain of her arms aching. But she washed every Monday, I daresay praying for a warm blustery day to dry it all quickly outside.

The Church was always somewhere Mum would look to for support. I'm not sure how well that worked for her at that time, as I was not yet 5, but life wasn't a stroll in the park.

Dad bought a record player and taught square dancing in the Church Hall for some extra cash one evening a week. I was aware at this time that life was quite hard, and particularly my mum worried about everything. Mum would often refer to being careful with money and not having lots to spend. She was very vocal about it. Communication wasn't such that anything would change that. We all know that can often be a normal household with three young children.

But eventually the time came when all the hard work was to pay off. We were able to buy a house just a few miles up the road. I remember looking at the dining chair in the corner of the room next to the door when I was told we were moving. I knew that chair and where it belonged. It was familiar to me and I took it for granted. It worried me I didn't know what moving that chair somewhere else would mean. Somewhere I didn't know. Where would I be?

It was 1962, the year of the bad winter when we moved to that three-bedroom semi-detached house in New Malden. I was now nearly five years old and it was the house my father would live in for fifty years till he died at ninety-one, and the house I would live in till I went to college at eighteen. It was an ok house. Standard three-bedroom semi. Same as. I don't remember where the chair went in the end. I suspect all was lost in the big move, of which I remember nothing. But perhaps even as a young child, when there's space in your mind, it allows you time to think. When exciting events happen, you're pulled along with them. When I say space, I wonder if in that chair moment, I needed some reassurance and love. I don't remember what I got, but I remember worrying about the chair.

As a six-year-old I went to a local Catholic school, where I met lots of friends, some of which I still know today. In those days I was given two pence to catch the bus home on my own a short way along the A3. A little quieter than it is now but still a main road. My mum knew how long it took for me to get home so was always expecting me on time. I remember once I walked back along the line of front garden brick walls, the ones that go up and down as they're laid. I remember this because I felt so guilty for not catching the bus, I left the two pence fare money on the wall so's not to be caught out. I was surprised when I got home to be told off severely. I hadn't realised even a short bus trip was much quicker than walking. Be fair, I was only six and pushing the boundaries.

CHAPTER 7

LIFE CHANGING

I met my mum's dad and my dad's mum when I was very young, and just about remember them. It was soon after that we didn't visit them anymore, so I had no relationship with them. I didn't know them, and they didn't know me. In the same way, I didn't know any of my aunts or uncles. All ten of them. It wasn't that I didn't know them because I didn't want to. They just weren't there to know. They weren't a part of my life. I was isolated from extended family connections.

At this age, I didn't know what people did. How often they saw each other, and what family relations were. It's hard to imagine family not being there when you have already experienced their presence and rolls. But when they're not there, it's hard to understand what's missing. These were all lost relationships because my mother was pulling away from both families for whatever reason she had in her head. And these were all voids that would eventually come back to smack me in the face in my adult life, when I would come to realise just what those supports were that I hadn't had, and how that made me different to most other people, and friends. I couldn't recall a family event, visit or anything similar like my friends, because we didn't have them. As time went on there were a couple of exceptions to this, when we went to organised parties for a specific celebration. I say 'we'. I mean not mum. She would not or could not go. It was dad's phone calls that quietly kept him in contact with their brothers and sisters, unbeknown to me at the time.

    In the new house we bought a fold up single bed in case we had any visitors staying overnight. It would live on the landing and have lots of bits and pieces put on it. There wasn't so much room now for the oil filled Dimplex radiator we all used to fight to get our clothes on in the winter months, so they were warm when we put them on in the morning. People talk now about being cold because

they can't put their heating on, and children need it on all night. We didn't have central heating for quite a while, but neither did most other people. That bed I would say must have been purchased with a very optimistic frame of mind. I don't remember it ever being used. Who was there to sleep in it. Who would visit?
I was aware of family disruptions but didn't think any more of them. They were accepted, presented as normal life and I knew no different.

At the time it didn't bother me much, though I was aware my mother had tensions with all of the East End family. Not because she was falling out with them, but she was isolating herself, and consequently us, in all directions. And that was the way it was to continue. It was to become a one-way road.

I had no aunts and uncles I saw, no relations at all that I had connections with let alone relationships. We had no family friends. We didn't go on days out, have parties, have any fun together as a family. Life was contained in a small dysfunctional unit. Birthday parties were unheard of after the age of six.

We were brought up to think we had to be careful with money. It had been a stretch living in Surrey with three young children before my dad had moved up in his company. Something which worried my mum. She was a worrier, and always was. It didn't help her state of mind working from a base of worry. But then, which came first? One consequence of this was my dad having to step in where mum might've otherwise been in control. I guess she would normally have her finger on the pulse rather than dad, when gauging ideas for us for Christmas presents, for example. Instead, that started to fall to dad, who with the best will in the world, and given he was working most of the time, wasn't quite up to speed as best he might. He once bought me a guitar for Christmas. It had The Beatles faces on it and was plastic. Several years earlier it might've been a good present. I was so upset that he didn't seem to have a clue where I was in my development and had bought me a baby present. I was aware life wasn't as it should be and I didn't have the understanding that went with that. Dad having to take on roles he wasn't prepared for in their partnership was hard for him. He was having to take on more than his fair share.

I don't know if he read my reaction, but I wasn't angry that I remember, just upset. Mum was retreating more into herself and leaving him to fill the gap. I suppose it felt like a breakdown in their relationship at this point, and dad was trying to smooth over the cracks without showing too much of a reaction. I don't think any of us knew where it would eventually lead, but were trying to take everything on board as best we could by accepting in a muted way.

The stress of the whole home situation started to hit dad hard. He was trying to earn a good wage for his family and keep his job down, whilst having to come home and take on other family responsibilities, which, frankly, were becoming too much for him.

One year I asked for a bike for my birthday with ideas of going trekking and exploring. I was lucky. I did get a bike. But one with little wheels and no gears. Not the mountain type of bike equivalent of today, or anything like that for which I could disappear off and explore on. Perhaps even share some experiences with my dad, but that was never going to happen.

Nobody had the space, or time, to listen to what I wanted or needed. It didn't make me feel angry, just upset and sad.

Christmas was one to miss. Again, we saw no relatives or friends. We couldn't invite any neighbours in as my mum would be in the front room, entirely unsociable and it was uncertain what she might do at any time, even more so if we had guests. We did get invited across the road to my friends' parents for a drink, and then to their neighbours, but we could never reciprocate. It was 'understood' my mother had had some sort of 'mental breakdown', and it was 'very sad'. She was hidden within the family, mostly unknown by outsiders.

We used to hang Christmas cards up on a string and had decorations hung from the centre light to each of the corners of the ceiling in the dining room and lounge. My dad used to pin them up. When I was big enough I used to help him, sometimes putting them up myself. Then it was just me putting them up. Eventually, if I didn't put them up, they didn't see the light of day. It was much the same with the Christmas tree. We used to like hanging lots of lametta on it. Being the youngest, the enthusiasm ran out before my wish to have a festive Christmas did. Hopes were always raised for me, and always dashed. There was one positive. It was traditional in our house to have a long table full of nuts and sweets for Christmas. That and mum would insist on having the coal fire burning at full blast. Every now and then a dive into the hall would be like jumping into an iced plunge pool. The heat relief was wonderful.

    And so life continues.

CHAPTER 8

BUT FIRST - PREP

I was only at my first school for a short while. My dad was doing quite well, and I was told I was going for an interview to a prep school in Wimbledon. I don't remember being particularly nervous. I think it was because I didn't really understand much of what it was about, apart from whether I was going to go to this school or not. I don't remember being told it was because I was clever. At the age of seven, it is perhaps more about educational choice than intelligence. Provided you could pass a basic interview, that is. It was just a different school and all the friends I'd met so far wouldn't be going there.

On this occasion that wasn't a problem. It would be my change of school after this that would be the life changing experience for me.

My dad must've had some time off work to take me to the interview. I was offered a place even though in the headlights of the moment of my first ever interview at seven years old, I couldn't remember both spellings of the words right and write.

The four years I spent at that school gave me the best start I could've had given the circumstances. A lot was expected of me, and discipline was strict, but that mostly worked for me. It gave me a structure I didn't have and an expectation I needed. I felt supported and looked after. It was a secure learning environment, which, on reflection, gave me a foundation to root myself for many years to come.

The first two years were in big classes where we learned the basics such as times tables and spellings. This time passed without event. Then, in the second two years, our classes were split in two, meaning half the pupils in a class, a much greater focus on each of us. But also, room for characters to stand out with their strengths. I was in the higher class of the two, but nearer the bottom, was the fastest sprinter in the school, sang in the choir and was made captain of the school rugby team in my last year. That was important. I was a leader, and we were a team. I felt good for that confidence.

The strength that built in me helped me survive events that were already happening and were to dominate parts of my life.

In those first two years, I don't remember what specifically was happening at home, except that life was changing. I don't remember much of my brother being there. We shared a bedroom, but I was usually asleep before he came to bed, and he was becoming a long-haired parka wearing mod on his Lambretta, and not home so much. But there was unhappiness as the next two years became difficult.

We used to go to church on a Sunday morning. As my dad wasn't religious, he would drive us there in our red Austin A40. My mum was always sat in the back, which unfortunately meant we fought for the front seat. These fights were upsetting and enough on occasion to prevent us from going at all. Everyday life was beginning to break down and become more strained, and as life was changing, Dad was having to suffer the constant barrage of abuse from mum. She was taking out all her frustrations on him.

As a couple, parents need each other's support to combat and share the stress life throws at you, connect the dots and manage particularly with young children. But that wasn't happening here. That would require being on the same page, even reading the same book, a scenario that was becoming an ever more distant reality. And if they were unable to work together, what message was that sending to the rest of us who needed the family structure. We were all having to find a way to manage.

On a Saturday morning, we would drive to Kingston, as it was the biggest local shopping centre. By this time my mother, sat in the back, would be gesturing to other drivers, often with two fingers and shouting things from inside the car. She was reading signs and signals and interpreting things going on around her as meaning something, specifically directed to her. Instructions she needed to pay attention to and follow. But they wouldn't be clear instructions. They would change, contradict, and confuse. Her anger and frustration becoming more apparent as they kept coming. Other drivers were the culprits with their brake lights and indicators, and she had no qualms in letting them know how she felt.

This type of behaviour was growing in its frequency and aggression. I remember the awkwardness, but I couldn't do anything to make it better. My dad would sometimes turn off the road to avoid that embarrassment and potential responses. Not everybody would understand what was going on. Probably nobody in fact. More a case of preventing an unwanted reaction. On reflection, I was in training for other things that were to come, behaviours to get used to, and finding a natural way of managing it all. It was obviously odd and unusual behaviour, but we all were learning to live and manage it. It wasn't a time to think about how my friends' mums live and behave. My world was too all-encompassing to try and imagine what I couldn't imagine. I just didn't know, and real time was filling my mind and emotions. There seemed no way to get through and communicate with mum. She was on her own journey in a parallel world, one nobody was invited into, just to experience. But neither could any help be got. There would be no cooperation from mum or even the opportunity to talk about the situation. You see, we were all in it too, she thought. Nobody knew anything about mental illness at this time, what could be done, or what it was all about. The unwritten brief was to manage it as best you could. There would be time much later before that reality when effects of these situations would impact on me.

CHAPTER 9

HOLIDAYS

I remember 1966 well. No guesses why I remember that year. I was nine years old. It was the last year we had a family holiday. That is one with my mother. I remember clearly how we started this holiday. I knew the plan, as much as there was one, was to take a long drive, find somewhere to stay, and have a holiday. Not the most comprehensive, but the first part of the plan was successful. As we left the back door of the house we were going to Devon. By the time we got to the back gate, some twenty yards away, we were going to Scotland. Or was it the other way round. Thereby lay the state of communication and harmony we were to expect for the duration.

I remember little about that holiday. Just that we never were able to find somewhere good enough by mum's standards to stop to eat, so chocolate bars and crisps were eventually bought. Might be considered a treat in some circumstances, but the route to that treat was fraught. I remember the World Cup on the radio as we drove along in the car. I remember hearts ice cream (too big for a child I was told). But of the holiday . . .

At home, my mum used to shop between two local centres nearby. Each a bus trip in opposite directions from our house, as she didn't drive. Certain days would be one direction and different shops, another day in the other. I got on a bus with her one day and she said to the driver, 'Take me where I need to go.' Of course, the driver looked at her with puzzlement, and I thought, well it only goes as far as Kingston! Her question was bizarre to anybody else. I wonder where my head was, but I do remember these times and her behaviour was just something to manage, but unpredictable.

My mother now was gradually slipping further into her own worries and world, becoming more paranoid in her thoughts and actions. I'm not sure when I ever felt the warmth and connection a child expects to feel from his mother, though I feel sure it must've been there in my very young years. But now I had an independence. Independence not because I was fighting for it as would normally be the case, but independence because everything else had retreated away and left me to manage on my own. I instinctively took hold of that independence as if it were a natural life progression. For me it was and had to be.

But for most children of that age, they were still in a supportive family environment. The difference allowed me to manage the world I had already been in for some time and was going to allow me to survive in the future.

That world would be the one, which I would eventually choose to describe the legacy of my childhood as, but it took me a few decades to realise.
'Survivor'.

In school holidays, I was always bored. On more than one occasion a week I would try persuading mum to let me have some money to go and buy myself a Vesta

Curry for two. They were dried curries of a type in sachets in a box. Easy to 'cook' and was a tasty lunch for me. Single portion was too mean for a young boy. I didn't always succeed because they were relatively expensive but kept me quiet for a while.

    I would look forward to watching BBC2 on the half hour every hour during the day. There wasn't any real daytime television in those days. They showed documentaries about nature or science. They were quite interesting first time round and helped to punctuate my days. I would spend time in the garden whizzing around on a three wheeled scooter with the rubber off one wheel, so it made a scraping noise as I swung it around the corners of the concrete path, leaving engrained scratches on it. I'd spend time bashing a tennis ball against the side of the garage wall, trying to miss the small glass window one side and the glass in the door the other. Not always successfully I hasten to add. And frequently having to get a ladder out of the garage to climb up on the corrugated, and probably asbestos roof to retrieve balls that I'd hit too far over the top, worrying our neighbour who would see me from her back window thinking I might fall through. It was a double garage, so half hers too. All was good to do, but I was bored. No parent to be a part of or help organise any other activity, event, trip, or just anything.

School time was better. I had made the choir at Prep school, I was the fastest runner in the school in the last years, I was good at art, and allowed to finish my work into the next lesson because it was one of the best. I was made captain of the school rugby team in my last year. I think my PE teacher might've thought it would be a good developmental decision to make me captain. If true he was right, and I owe Mr O'D a debt of gratitude. If not, I still owe him the same because he built me some strength and a voice so vital for me at that stage. He was always directing me about how I should lead and manage the team. I still believe this was the

best rugby I was to ever play. Big hearted team members pulling together, wanting to win. As I learnt I would shout at the team. Keep them on their toes, in the right place at the right time. On their case. So much so I remember some opposition teams complaining because my vocal persistence would put them off. It was an unusual tactic, but hey I'll take that.

In my last prep year, I was also made prefect. I was not to find this out until a few days before term. The letter informing us had been posted and received at home, but my mother had hidden it. She was now of the mind that we, her family, were not meant to succeed. Things were already taken care of and just as she couldn't be successful in her paranoia, reading messages given to her, neither were we able to succeed. Now there was no point in having ambition or wanting encouragement. Because now it was all out of our hands. Others were making the decisions, and we were destined not to succeed. Much as I knew this was her illness talking, it was hard not to feel as if my legs had just been taken away from underneath me. Much as I knew it was her illness talking, she was still the parent I expected encouragement and belief from.

My mother was very strong, if that's the correct interpretation, and entered into the battle in full force. I sit here recounting these events, 'blowing out' wells of emotion. My mother would sit in the front room, her eyes red and teary for hours on end, trying to manage the world around her. This was not our world, my world, it was entirely the tormented world in which she lived.

Once the letter making me a prefect was discovered, and I'm not sure how, we could see the preparations required for me before the first day of school in the new academic year. One important and very visual part was to have braid sewn around the edge of my blazer designating prefect. My dad did his best to get the braid and other things required to sew on for the first day. But there wasn't much time because of mum's secrecy, and I had to go to school without.

First, my friends thought I hadn't been made prefect. Then some thought I would be but why didn't I have things sorted. At that age of ten years old having to explain was such a difficult thing. Truth couldn't be told. But then what do you say? They wouldn't understand, I knew that. There is no easy way. To be ashamed my parents couldn't get together what all the other caring and attentive parents had done with ease for me was so upsetting. And, of course, there's that look - the first response from teachers. I had a letter somehow explaining, but so what. The headmaster, who a few years previously had given me the ferula (a leather strap across the palm of my hand) for being a bit naughty, dropped his stern exterior that moment in his office, stood next to me and put his arm around my shoulders while I briefly burst into tears. A moment for me to express my upset and for him to warmly acknowledge it. Instead of feeling proud of myself for my last year, the moment had been sucked away. It wouldn't be the first time, or the last.

Only now has it occurred to me to wonder what exactly my dad wrote in that letter. How did he explain the situation? Was he open and honest about it? I'm not so sure.

But somehow, I understood it was not my mother's fault. Fault wasn't the issue. Blame wasn't the issue. I wasn't angry, I was just upset. I was just a boy trying to live a boy's life. Making things right and getting through was the only option, though I wasn't aware that was what I was doing. I was feeling starved, a void, but I was surviving.

CHAPTER 10

SQUASHED

I can remember the exact date, it was 8 December, 1968. Lunchtime. I was walking along the cycle track beside the A3. Not such a busy road in those days, but still a dual carriageway. There was snow on the ground and I was messing around on the adjacent pavement with my friend.

'Watch out for that truck,' he shouted.

As I turned quickly, I slipped, my right leg stretched out on the cycle track just as a flatbed council gritting lorry was driving past at normal speed. Not gritting. The back wheels rolled over the bottom of my leg. My instant reaction of shock was to grab my leg and hold it tight, rolling around in the snow for what seemed like ages.

I could feel a strange tingling and numbness in my leg. I didn't want to let it go in case . . . in case . . . I didn't know. I didn't know what was going to happen.

Home was about a quarter of a mile away, so my friend rushed to get my mum. An ambulance was called, and mum came rushing down, panic and worry on her face. A second ambulance arrived, take note, and I was whisked off to Kingston Hospital. It wasn't until I was waiting on a bed in a hospital corridor that the shock broke and emotion overwhelmed me. I was put under anaesthetic and had twenty-four stitches down the inside of my calf. Luckily with the snow cushioning the ground and being young with a little flex in my bones, I did not break my leg. Instead, the weight of the truck split my calf down most of its length.

I can remember the ambulance men cutting away my trousers. They were cut and thrown away as there were some little bits of flesh from my leg still trying to hang on. They were my favourite trousers and I had worn them day in and day out. They were a light beige colour and unfortunately showed the dirt a little too easily for a ten-year-old boy. I think mum couldn't have come in the ambulance with me. I guess she needed to be home for when my brother and sister came back from school. But dad was there when I came to and had my plaster on.

By the time the rugby season was on I was back on track.

I got through my last year at Prep School. Life was becoming more of a challenge.

Thankfully, rugby practice was most evenings in the winter with a game Wednesday afternoon and Saturday morning. I really enjoyed the team element of playing rugby. I guess it was the only positive team experience I was having and I indulged in it.

In my last year as part of our homework, we often had to learn four lines of poetry, and repeat them as we went around the class next morning. It was something I hated. There was nobody to help at home and my head was too full and unclear even for such a simple thing to remember even four lines and I was often caught out next day.

I have one lasting memory and consequence of my mum when I was at Prep School.

It was early spring I guess; the end of the rugby season and a Saturday was set aside for house teams to play in a tournament Sevens Rugby. Naturally, as captain of the school team, I was captain of the first team in my house Loyola, and we stood a good chance of winning the competition. It was my last year at this school, so was an event I was looking forward to. At this stage, there was a lot of competitiveness amongst us and pride in what we had played together. It was going to be a good day. I got up that morning primed for the competition. In my experience since, the last year of junior school is always one of the best. We were year six, top of the tree, brimming with confidence, and ready before being put in our place again come secondary school after the summer holidays.

At home, my brother had passed his driving test and was allowed, on occasion, to drive my dad's company car. Without telling my dad, mum had sent my brother out to the shops to buy something. I was getting ready to go to my rugby competition . . . but there was no car to get me there.

I stepped back, concerned about what was happening while circumstances unfolded. He was gone, the car was gone, and I was due to leave for the competition. The temperature was rising and so were the voices. When did he leave? How long would he be? Would he come straight back? Why did you send him? Mum was unaware of my big day. The argument raged on. Eventually a taxi was called in the hope we could get there in time before my first game.

But by the time I got to the ground the tournament had started. If I were to join in and play at all now it had to be for the second team as the firsts had been made up due to my absence. I was so upset as I changed. Some friends came in, seeming to understand how I felt. But I was ashamed firstly to have let everyone down, and secondly to miss that big final moment at my school doing something I enjoyed and was good at, expecting it to be such a high.

    At the end of my time at this school, came the 11 plus. This was the entrance exam for grammar school. The natural progression would be to pass this exam and follow my friends across the road to the Grammar school. Failing would mean having to go to a different school without them. I felt pretty good about the exam and was thinking I had done quite well. So, it was a shock to me when I found out I had failed. I was upset and protested at home, not wanting to accept the result. So much so we had it checked, but somehow, I had managed to fail. At first there was the shame. There was a hollowness for me as to who I was because I hadn't managed to achieve the same as my peers. I don't remember anyone else failing.

It exacerbated my feeling of separation from them, which because of my home life, was already there for me. I was having to identify with my circumstances and not my vision. This event, result, seemed to make public the truth of my experiences. I was clawing at trying to keep with the norm, but this would force the difference. They had passed and would move on together, whereas I would have to go to another school on my own. Again, I was on my own. And then there was home. I was the youngest of three, and the only one to have failed.

And so, much as I appreciated the huge value that school gave me, and the tools to move on, my head was down, and I felt alone. Not really understanding what was happening around me, but just living through and surviving the experience.

CHAPTER 11

THERE ON THE STAIR

I was upset and unhappy. Life was still very difficult as I sat at the top edge of the stairs. It was just somewhere to be. I sat with my back to the mirror on the wall and from there I could see into my bedroom and my parent's bedroom. At the back of their room was my father's wardrobe and on top were two suitcases. The one on the nearest edge was a tatty old blue one with soft sides, and quite small. That was enough for me, I thought.

I wanted to leave home.

I couldn't think of why I would want to stay. Not only would it be an escape, but perhaps it might also be a way for me to show how unhappy I was. I don't know if anybody knew that. There was no avenue to express myself, no one to express my feelings to. And I didn't even understand that. It wasn't because people didn't care but because they were all in it too, all of us occupied with our own ways of coping.

What I didn't realise at that time was that home did give me some security. Not from my family to me, but that I had somewhere dare I say it, 'safe and secure' to live, and we had enough money. Not the stuff you really think about before your early teens.

In my mind I was thinking – where would I go?

Family was all too far away, but we had no contact with them anyway. I didn't know them. We had no family friends, anyone I could trust or confide in. Anyone full stop. The realisation of isolation from family and friends and the consequences of that were beginning to hit home. I would be out on the street. And then I started to think what would I achieve? I felt alone. Where could I go?

My home and family life had made me see things with a responsibility. And that person in me was telling me it was most sensible to stay put and carry on. I would only end up being brought back here again. I had no understanding of what help there might be out there. I had no confidence there was any. And I knew I would embarrass my dad and cause problems where there were already plenty. He had told me to try not to argue, and just manage the situation.

Perhaps, if there had been violence, obvious physical abuse, danger which I could readily identify my instinct would make me run, not sit and think about it. But it wasn't like that. It was numbing. There was a gradual weight of trying to manage, find somewhere to put all the troubles. There wasn't that instant reaction. In a way, it was how I was being taught, educated. To grow up managing all the issues. I was too young to do all the analysis. But I was never too young to know how it made me feel.

And so, I put what looked like my grown up hat on, wherever that came from, still feeling upset and trapped, and made a conscious decision that I would remember this moment. That decision felt so very important to me. I felt that, at some point, it would be important to recall this moment, to remember just where I was in my thoughts at that time. That it was real because I didn't understand. I felt lifeless. I never imagined that moment would be now, more than fifty years later. I looked back at the view of the case on my dad's wardrobe from where I was sitting on the stairs and remembered how low I was feeling. I didn't want to forget how I felt that day because stay or go would dictate how life would be in the coming years.

CHAPTER 12

THE WRONG FORK IN THE PATH

And, so to secondary school. A Catholic Secondary Modern School. Failing the eleven plus meant that a grammar school was out of the question.

There was an option to wear short trousers . . . to secondary school . . . first year.

Mum said why not. I said never. Who in their right mind would start a new secondary school in shorts? Not only that but everybody, bar a handful at best, were going to be wearing long trousers. The new boys were going to get picked on anyway. It would be like shining a light on yourself saying, 'Look at me I'm a wally!' Embarrassment wouldn't even cover it. Even putting it in as an option was cruel. I eventually won the argument, but it was a struggle. I spent the first two years in this school doing quite well. I should have. I had been pushed hard in my last school and so was ahead of my contemporaries. I had some slack so could stay near or at the top of the class in every subject that was in sets ability. The PE teacher took one look at me and asked me why I was there. It wasn't helpful to feel I didn't fit in when I already felt I shouldn't be there, when all my friends were at a different school. At a reunion some years later, a few ex-pupils remembered they thought I didn't really fit in. The style of education and level of discipline was so different.

This move for me educationally was the worst thing that could possibly happen. I had left a method of education, which worked in a different way. One which I had been trained into and which worked for me. I had been taken away from my friends at the age of eleven and put into a different system altogether. It wasn't a bad school, far from it. But the change was a mistake for me, and I didn't have the support or the space to see me through it. I don't think my parents understood what that meant. Perhaps they had invested in me at Prep School, and I had disappointed. Education now was a mile away from their experiences in the East End where not surprisingly their formal education finished in their mid-teens at best. Completely.

In my first years, I was in a friendship group of three. I was to come to realised later that three's allowed me to be an outsider of the group. I did the same thing in later school years with another group of three friends. I was more comfortable to be able to stay on the fringe if I wanted. It was a pattern coming from my earlier experience. How do you explain your homelife, family life, how you're feeling, why you're upset to one of your peers who you know has no experience of why or how you're feeling? It was a pattern I only partly, and quite naturally evolved to protect myself of being the focus by being slightly on the outside, but still being as much a part of the friendship group as I could be.

For a while, I used to bus into Kingston on a Saturday, go into Bentalls Department Store and ask for broken candles from their candle stall. They sold them cheap and I would melt them down in an old brown enamel saucepan in my bedroom on a calor Gaz camping stove. The little blue stove, quite dangerous with a heavy metal saucepan on top. I don't think anybody really registered what I was doing in terms of safety and burning the house down. Maybe, I would be the first person in the house to have a leg wax! Or it just wasn't important enough in the grand scheme of things at the time. The carpet was a bit of a mess anyway. I'd hang a bit of string in the centre of an old plastic bottle and pour the melted wax in. A slight melting of the bottle from the heat would give the candle its own individual look. I was quite successful, making coloured layers and patterns, until I discovered I could buy wax from the chemist in a block. I could up my production I thought and Bentalls were getting a bit fed up with seeing my face every week. They just didn't break that many candles. My brother had sold a few of my candles to his mates at University as the design was very trendy at the time. The only problem was the wax the chemist sold was paraffin wax. I wasn't aware the melting point of paraffin wax was much lower than the type used in candles. Well not until my brothers mate was asking for his money back because his candle had melted all over the table. The novelty was wearing off. Such creative skills weren't to be woken up again until I discovered you could make wine out of just about anything, including tea, when I was in my last years of school.

After a few years I use to cycle to school. I now could ride my brothers old racing bike, but I wasn't allowed to ride to school on it. If I was quick, I could escape before mum could see me and so could leave myself fifteen minutes and be in on time. In my older years, I had trumpet lessons at school and played second trumpet at assembly. The advantage being I could get in later than everyone else, pick up my 'cold' trumpet and slip in the front of assembly without anyone noticing. As a teenager, you'll understand, I could roll out of bed just before nine and be in assembly ready to play by quarter past. Some bum notes could've been heard from a cold trumpet if it weren't for the first trumpeter, who was very, very good. Good enough for me on occasion, to mime to . . .

By third year work was suffering. Why wouldn't it? No push for two years meant a flunk in third and fourth, and eventually fifth, by which time geography on a Friday morning was spent around my girlfriend's house. I can't complain about my teachers. Others did well. But I was like a feather floating slowly down in the breeze, hoping not to land in a puddle . . . or worse.

I was beginning to wish that my parents would separate. Not a happy thought, but separation would be better than the constant arguing and unhappiness at home. I guess I still thought of myself as normal in a way and hadn't really registered at this point that this was more than an unhappy marriage, but the consequence and depth mental illness brings to relationships. Perhaps, we all want to seem normal to hide the truths. It's a way to survive.

    I would sometimes take myself off to Kingston, by the power station as it used to be on the River Thames next to Kingston Bridge. There were a few benches, and the area was quiet, not many people around. A little oasis amongst the hustle of the surrounding town. It felt a good place to think, to reflect. But it never seemed to give me solace. I would leave feeling much the same as I had arrived and that frustrated me. I realise now why that was. I didn't need the reflection, I needed something else. I didn't need to be on my own with my thoughts. I needed something else. I needed engagement with the problems. I needed to understand properly what was happening to me and where I was. I needed someone who was a part of this story to communicate with, understand and share what we were all having to deal with. Not be doing it in isolation. Isolation had already been the most dangerous device which predicated this. But then mental illness and isolation are old friends.

Isolation isn't only evident in this type of mental illness. When you think of abuse in partner relations, especially with children involved. The abusive partner would often want to move house, perhaps away from the victim's family and friends. Detach them from that support and survival structure they would naturally need and depend on. Using that isolation as a means of control to prevent intrusion or influence from outside. But whether isolation is used to manipulate, or is a consequence of an illness, it will always be a weapon.

About this time my dad contracted Bell's Palsy. An illness, which temporarily paralysed and dropped one side of his face. This distressed my dad but was likely a response to the stress and strain he was under at work, and with no respite at home either. He also got chicken pox as well as shingles. He was having to survive too.

My dad did organise a doctor to call on my mother. Perhaps he now thought there might be something that could be done to help. It would've been a big step to accept he needed to ask a doctor to intervene. I don't exactly remember what prompted him to do this. I was unlikely to be a part of that conversation, but I did know it was going to happen, and of course why. It was the first occasion that I knew mum's mental state was to be properly recognised by anybody, including our family. The first time anything was being done to acknowledge it. As is still the case, a patient has to be willing to see or accept treatment from a doctor, unless in an emergency of course. When mental illness is involved, there is more of a problem. If the patient doesn't consider there is anything wrong due to their mental state, or that there is an emergency, they will clearly not cooperate. Then the only choices are to section if evidence justifies, or step back.

My mum answered the door. The doctor introduced himself. She said no thank you and closed the door on him. End of story.

Comprehension of such mental health problems in the sixties and seventies was next to nothing. Without any consent from the patient the doctor had no choice but to leave.

Home had various stages. A good meat and two veg was served most evenings at this time, though that eventually stopped. I don't remember when. It's hard to describe what sort of character or who mum was. There was no honest conversation with her which is hard to imagine in somebody as a constant, especially your mother. The person she once was, before this story, was never present. I was never really interacting with my mum since then but the world she occupied and protected. The bandwidth was taken with coping behaviour on all sides. I can't explain her personality. It wasn't there to be seen except to say she was

tenacious in her independent mind. But not a normal personality to be seen. Nothing to relate to. I didn't know her.

Dad was never home early from work weekday evenings. Always came in late, around tenish, with an *Evening Standard* and sometimes could fall asleep on his feet in the lounge inside the door and next to the TV. His most remarkable talent. He would dangerously sway on his feet as he nodded off. He would then sit and eat a long-warmed dinner cooked at the same time as ours some three or four hours before. And he would always eat it.

In my younger teens, I wanted to please my dad. I often would cut the grass in summer and dig the garden. The neighbours would comment as they walked past as most teenagers wouldn't be quite so helpful. I would get a thank you from my dad, so would do it often. But no extra pocket money. I was wanting to do more jobs to give myself the opportunity to earn more, but he wasn't having any of that. Seemed to me he was stifling my entrepreneurial instincts. But it did give me something to do, keep me occupied so I wouldn't get bored.

I used to open the garage doors so he could drive his car straight in when he got home. He wouldn't always be home before I went to bed, but I could hear his car coming down the road. He would sometimes fall asleep at the wheel outside the garage and eventually wake up and come in. He had a talent to fall asleep anytime, anywhere. A practicing narcoleptic.

I once creosoted all the garden fence for him, ending up unwell in bed for several days. Nobody had mentioned holding the can to me as I painted meant I was constantly breathing in the fumes.

I wasn't really aware too much there were things which should happen on a regular basis like going to the dentist. It didn't worry me that I hadn't been in ages. I didn't particularly like going. My dentist had a glass eye and wasn't very good with children. I can vouch for that. Were they ever in those days? I don't know.

I must've been in my early teens when my brother was home from university, and he spotted me at the dinner table using a flat ended dinner knife to get some meat out a big hole in my back tooth. He was appalled. I wasn't. It didn't hurt and I had no concept of what was supposed to happen when it came to such matters. My parents would buy a large bottle of coke – full fat – and a big packet of crisps every weekend for my sister and I. Oh and cream cakes! Clearly a recipe for disaster teeth wise, though thoroughly enjoyed at the time and still do. I don't remember if I cleaned my teeth as I should. I suspect not.

My brother had left home for university and so his experiences were obviously from an earlier time, as well as now seeing events from a distance as they progressed. As you would think, he was clearly in a different place. Not necessarily better, I don't know, but less exposed to the immediate effect of living with mum now. Talking and sharing about home life didn't happen much between my dad and me or my brother and sister. We were each experiencing home life in different ways and managing in our own ways too. We had a common challenge, but surviving that challenge was individual. Hence much as our experiences were strongly linked, there was little discussion.

Living standards were deteriorating in our household. I was not aware.

Why would I be? But I was experiencing them.

Mum's behaviour was becoming more difficult and controlling of the home space. There was a long period when my mum would be sitting on the edge of her seat, mostly trying to look out of the big bay window and down onto the road. Our house was set a little back from the road and the front garden was raised a bit. She was on the constant look out for whatever signal she was expecting. It seems like she had some language of what she was reading, except when she thought she knew what a sign, a flashing light perhaps or a plane would happen, then something else would tell her there was another thing to watch for, or the signal went off and would mean the opposite. She would get so angry at the mixed signalling, change of direction, change of message and she would shout at the world outside in her anger. She would get up from the sofa, looking out of the lounge window, and go into the hall and put her hat and coat on. Sometimes just go to the front door. Sometimes open it, sometimes go outside, sometimes walk up and down the front path, and sometimes up and down the road a little. Almost every time she did this she would come back, take off her hat and coat, maybe come back into the lounge and then repeat another of those variations. It was tiring to watch, exhausting to experience every day, every evening.

    This simple but impossible scenario would go on for hours and days. Weeks even. She was totally absorbed and drowned in what she couldn't escape from. It was perpetual motion and so would never end. Couldn't end because it was her own production line. The only reason I can account this detail is because she would shout her frustration as it was happening.

The behaviour bore no relation to anything outside her world. It was not for any other effect or reason but for what was going on in her own head. The pull of her world over rode everything else to the point that eventually she had a bowl in the corner of the room to pee in, as she couldn't not be there and miss something vital, that signal. Eventually we realised too that she was hearing voices. She was being teased, tormented. Nothing ever came to an end for her. Go here, go there, do this, do that. Of course, from the outside there could be no conclusion. There was nothing to conclude. If there was everything would go away. It was self-fulfilling. The perfect storm. But that is what we were dealing with and what this sort of mental illness is about. There is no way to communicate or intervene into that vicious circle.

And so as is now evident, personal hygiene was a problem, and not an easy one to resolve. I don't remember how we moved on from there. Perhaps she developed into a different phase. Mum's teeth hadn't been looked after for many years. Not something I would've registered at the time unless it came up in conversation. I don't remember dad going to the dentist either, but I guess he did. If I had a hole in mine, well what was left of hers were quite simply blackened. Gaps around the gums where they were rotting and black. A wonder that she wasn't in great pain and discomfort, though who would know if she was. It wasn't something I ever heard her complain about.

What are the 'negative symptoms' of schizophrenia?

The term 'negative symptoms' is used to describe symptoms that involve loss of ability and enjoyment in life.
- *Lack of motivation*
- *Losing interest in life and activities*
- *Problems concentrating*
- *Not wanting to leave your house*
- *Changes to your sleeping patterns*
- *Not wanting to have conversations with people* • *Feeling uncomfortable with people*
- *Feeling that you haven't got anything to say*
- *Losing your normal thoughts and feelings*
- *No energy*
- *Poor grooming or hygiene*

Rethink Mental Illness

One school day, early in the week, one of my friends came home for a while. Always a risk. Because mum was controlled by this state of mind, she always had to be vigilant. At this point she wouldn't leave the front room. As I walked down the hall, by the lounge, mum opened the door a sliver so she could talk quietly to me. It was as if someone else might hear her. Through the crack of the door, she wanted me to go and buy something from the shop. I feel part of her still felt guilty in the back of her mind at not being able to carry out the duties she expected of herself as a mum and housewife. Her world was split in two. Guilt of what she knew she should be doing, and control from her masters.

I was used to her behaviour. That in itself kind of made me odd. But it was just the way she was. But to my friend that was weird.

I would nearly always go elsewhere to my friends. There were times mum would ask me to go to the local chemists to buy sanitary products for her. She would give me a note with the details on it so I could just hand it to the lady in the shop. It didn't bother me; guess I didn't really know much of what it meant or perhaps the stigma attached to it. But often I would get a strange look from the shop assistant. One night a week I would have to take the laundry down the road on my bike and do it at the laundrette. She would plead if I didn't want to, or couldn't, for some reason.

As a growing teenager I was naturally working through my own life. Mostly under my own steam. I gained a reputation at home for being bad tempered, shouting and slamming doors. A reputation, which is sometimes still attached to me to this day. From where I stood though, to my mind I thought is it any wonder! It never felt to me like a bad temper. I was a teenager frustrated as hell and there was nowhere for me to go with it. Dad not at home or receptive to me, mum a nutty brick wall. No communication or understanding. No relatives or family to talk to . . . to talk to me. No wonder I shouted and slammed doors with rage.

The most effect it had was on our semi-detached neighbour. She was a lovely lady, and never complained. She used to be a publican and didn't seem to be fazed by anything. From short conversations with my dad she knew something of what was going on in our house, though I have no idea how my dad would have told the story. She occasionally made some comment, but never in a disparaging way, but with some warmth and understanding. That was so lovely. That simple understanding. There were few people in my life at that time of whom I took notice. Because they were the markers for me as to where my life was separate to other more normal homes. It was only a small sense, perhaps something I might've got from extended family being around had they been there, but it gave me just a little perspective. That for me was valuable. I would sometimes see her looking at me with empathy and understanding. For that I saw her as a real person because there was an acknowledgement.

Her husband was ill, and she cared mostly for him at home. Once or twice, she'd pop in at Christmas and have a drink with us. Sometimes knocking on the window on her way across the gardens to say she could escape for a little while. Time enough for a quick whisky . . . or two! We knew nothing would bother her so we could be relaxed. She was a character, and we would always have a laugh. Simple things, which, again, I would always remember.

You know you can be more relaxed when someone has some understanding of your predicament, or it just didn't matter. That applied to us all.

But, another time, I was in the kitchen with mum, and I was a teenager challenging and shouting, as she would shout back. Or was it the other way round? In my frustration I knocked the kitchen table, which was in the middle of the room, with my knee. It was a jolt with real frustration, a reaction and it hit my mum in the leg. She always bruised easily, and she looked at me saying, 'You did that on purpose.' She was upset. My frustration was through the roof, and I was upset at what I'd done. There was no escape from some of these situations. There were no answers. Perhaps my dad's advice of 'try not to argue with her' was best. Well, in a dream world maybe. But where do you put all the stuff that's going on when the cupboards already full of junk!? When the door was opened, some stuff had to fall out. It was better to be out. Just out.

These were some of her more depressed and low times in that period. Weakened by the experience physically, but mentally always trying to follow whatever she was meant to do. Her behaviour changed many ways over these few years. Nothing was consistent. I would be woken up in the mornings, as a teenager in school holidays, with her shouting angrily at the top of her voice - defiant . . . to her world.

She wanted to learn to drive a car. Instantly, that put us all on alert as she was so reactive at that time. Her anger gave her strength. I remember talking to my sister about how we believed in her physical strength. If she decided to do something, physical ability wouldn't be the thing that stopped her. But she was very clear. If she had a car, she could drive herself into a brick wall and end it all. We found she had bought a stilson, a very large wrench, for the purposes of undoing the gas pipes and gassing us all. To her, that was helping us too by finishing us all off. That was how her torment had pushed her. She felt that was the only way out. I carried with me the reality of this drama. The possibilities of these events felt all too likely and real.

I will always remember sitting in class in third or fourth year, I remember the teacher. We called him Floss. After a knock on the door, a pupil came into the class to give Floss a written message. Because of these events, the first thing that shot straight into my mind was it might be a message for me, telling me mum had succeeded in killing herself. That was the first place I went in my thoughts. That is how much of my mind space was taken up emotionally, whilst concerned about and living with someone close to me who was suffering with such mental illness. Mum then went from being aggressive to emotionally drained and upset. She was a tormented soul, and she could do nothing about it. Because 'they' wouldn't let her. And neither could we help.

There is no way of changing a person's perception when they are mentally ill paranoid and deluded. No way to persuade them otherwise.

It is, was an impossible scenario.

I had some very good teachers in secondary school. I only wish I had the presence and focus to take advantage of them all. One was a lady who joined the staff in her first post and was to teach drama, a new subject at the school. A little like rugby in prep school this was a subject that would help me explore something quite different in myself. An opportunity to be more extrovert than introvert. Even expressive at times. Allowing me to be outside of myself. I wasn't going to get carried away, but it was good. Something I hadn't experienced in myself, but a move in the right direction for me, and one that I could only benefit from. It was a chance comment from 'Floss' suggesting I attend the drama club that initially helped, encouraged me to make that leap.

In my fifth year, we put on a production of *Boys in Brown*, a Borstal story. By this time, my hair was very long, way past my shoulders and much longer than anyone else at school. Not quite sure how I got away with it, but somehow managed to be quietly invisible to staff. Now where have I heard that notion before . . . there will be some reading this who will recognise what that means. Times when you feel you can make yourself disappear. At home the hair was easy. My brother broke the ground several years before with his 'mod' haircut. By the time child number three came round there was no appetite or interest in saying anything very much. So in line with most other things at that time. I have a photo still of me sat in a chair looking like King Charles II.

A play about borstal boys wasn't going to be easy with long hair, so I finally decided to get it cut and stuff the remainder under a wig. Not long after I decided to take the plunge and go for a normal haircut. The halfway house just didn't work.

At around the same time, a new centre had opened up in the local community called The Brycbox, a drama and arts centre for local students based on The Cockpit in London. There were classes for schools during the day and also during the evening for teenagers. It became quite a social centre as well as an opportunity to do something different. I was never at home during the evenings, nor ever wanted to be, and The Brycbox was a frequent destination, followed by the pub across the road. Occasionally, I might see my neighbour in the pub too.

We put on a second show at school called *Oh what a Lovely War,* which proved very popular especially with an older audience, as it still invoked distant memories of the First Word War. We were all booked out and squeezed as many in as we could. We needed some girls for this production too, so partly through the benefits of The Brycbox, we teamed up with a group from Tiffin Girls. It was a great success. I enjoyed the activity and the social life and was a tool to develop and distract myself.

My last few years of school were the most fun and at a pivotal time for me. I was involved in lots of drama, including helping teach the juniors on a Saturday morning at The Brycbox. As a school group we had lots of trips to see shows in the West End, something which would have never otherwise have happened. This opened me up and gave me a base of enjoying theatre and the arts, which, I thankfully hold on to till this day. It became the base for the next part of my education.

As a young adult home was never a place I wanted to be. I was out just about every evening. I had a local friend who went to the other boys' secondary school in town. As sociable teenagers, between us we just about knew everyone we came across. With both schools under our belts, in our evenings we visited all the youth clubs, which were mostly church clubs in the area, and as a pair we enjoyed each other's company. He was annoyingly talented and good at just about everything he did, from cooking to sewing to music, and was good looking to boot. We had the first dinner party (at his house of course) at I think sixteen or seventeen. Naturally, he was the cook, and his background was Asian, so it was a most delicious and successful evening.

As mates, we didn't talk much about problems. He was a sensitive and caring friend but there was an acknowledgement stuff was there, and that was enough. In fact, that was great. New and refreshing for me.

For those last two or three years before college my social life was more active than most others at that age, as was confirmed to me in due course. I had a big crowd of friends, and some lovely girlfriends through that period, as did many of my contemporaries. And certainly, in the last year went to parties most days of the weekends. Oh, how generous those parents were to give up their houses for a Friday or Saturday evening.

But that wasn't all that was going on. The same issues were happening at home. They still affected me; I was just able to remove myself from them more and exercise my own self. I was becoming more independent. What home offered me was diminishing. Maybe I was just coming to realise I wasn't missing a home at all. Yes, it offered me the security of a roof over my head, but emotionally I wasn't missing anything. But I hadn't yet properly realised what I had missed out on.

I remember sitting with my last girlfriend I had before going to college. We were in her room, and I was upset about something, but I couldn't explain what. I didn't understand it. I don't remember how it came about. Perhaps I felt overwhelmed. She tried to talk to me, but I couldn't respond. I was in a kind of emotional freeze. I couldn't explain or get out of it. She was very supportive and kind to me and tried to encourage me to talk. Eventually saying she couldn't help unless I said something. I couldn't and neither could I rescue myself from that feeling. She knew something of my homelife, but how do you open up when there is a flood of upset to let through first.

Perhaps the challenge of growing up with a parent with mental illness is that at first you take on the problems that affect you emotionally automatically as we all do in some way. Then, you take on more because that is the path you've been given until maybe you realise that these are problems. If you are too young, or are with no support, you have nowhere to go with them, so you carry on. Maybe you don't realise you need support. Either way the path only climbs uphill. The weight piles up beside your path, and your view either side is becoming obscured. Nobody can see how difficult the climb of this path is becoming because you are the only one on it, and there is no solution and only one direction. You feel overwhelmed. Where you've come from or how high you've climbed, there is no choice of direction. Your path carries on and it is beyond help and support because nobody has seen where it comes from or understands what it is about. And so you eventually climb to the top of that path. When you look out one way there is a beautiful valley, reaching far and wide. Abundant freedom and life. But turn behind you and see the dam of emotion, upset and feelings that have built up. You cannot really enjoy that beautiful view behind you until all that dam of emotion has been managed and has flowed through.

CHAPTER 13

A CAREER PERHAPS

Each stage in my life, I gained a little more independence and understanding, as one would expect. It never meant I could forget my mother and all that entailed, but as I experienced other people more, I realised how different my life was. And as I already understood how everything had affected me, I was about to realise that I had a whole new other experience to understand. Other people weren't quite the same as me. I was different.

I already knew my experiences were different, but now I was coming to realise that 'I' was different. I saw and did things differently to others. There was good and bad in that. Because of the exposure I had to all sorts of behaviours and situations and their consequences, I felt I was much more perceptive than most, and by definition, broader minded and understanding of various situations and events.

The separation of going to college was a break from how I existed before. I had gone from home life and all its issues, to making a big step and being grown up, and independent. It was a shock to me, and I had to reassess. It became the hardest continuous element of my life for many years, even decades.

I worked a little at Richmond Theatre, crewing backstage before I went to college but carried on doing 'get ins' and 'get outs' at weekends for extra cash as and when I could. I worked behind the college union bar a few nights a week, earning rather than spending, serving rather than drinking, and keeping in touch with everything going on. Friday night was favourite, as often there was a band playing and the bar would be four deep all night.

I had various relationships at college, as you do. Some for a while, others not so long. Lots of students were exploring their new freedoms. I felt I'd come in having had some lovely relationships before and a busy social life so I often felt I was in a different place to many, for whom those freedoms were very new.

Green King Abbot was the beer, quite strong for a session beer, not that it stopped anyone. That was when bitter was still the favoured beer to drink rather than lager. In my third year I decided I should drink Guinness. I felt that just in case I wasn't eating a healthy diet, I should play safe and drink Guinness. 'It's good for you'. I had started to make my own wine at home in the last year or so before college, trying everything from tea wine to banana wine in that same bedroom the candles were made. Instead of burning the place down, there was now more chance of blowing it up with some very messy fermentative explosions. My sister had a boyfriend, whose job seemed to supply him with many bananas, from which I made several gallons of wine. But in my first year at college I would always have a few bottles of blackberry wine in my boot to drink in someone's student garden.

But I got through college. Choosing to train as a teacher was something that I could possibly do. The only support or advice I had to get there was from my school drama teacher.

At that time for this course, we did a teaching practice each of the three years. You can imagine the first when you had only been in college a short while, was challenging. Sixth form pupils might be less than a year younger.

My third year and last school visit was challenging. I didn't understand why so much of my job was to control rather than teach, and the school discipline structure wasn't very supportive. My tutor from college came to assess. Now, the previous summer was the very warm one of '76, and we were lucky enough to have an outdoor swimming pool on our college campus, which was originally an old mansion house. Temptation got the better of me on one or two occasions, and I fell in the pool on my way to some psychology lectures. Unluckily for me, my psychology lecturer was now my examiner at this school. She had identified my absence and was about to make my life a little more complicated than I'd would have liked. So, it wasn't going too well, and it wasn't going to get any better.

It would be unfair of me to say I was being picked on in any way, but I was failed pending an external examiner. Suffice to say if there were a little wriggle room there, I feel it wouldn't have wriggled in my favour. Within a few days the external examiner turned up and was to sit through two of my lessons. The first with a class who were challenging, and the second with a class who were great. I passed by the skin of my teeth. I only had to get through the final exam now. And I'm sure the few beers in the bar the night before clinched it by relieving the pressure and allowing me to relax into a positive frame of mind for the exam next day.

And so, I left college not knowing what to do next. I had Qualified Teacher Status in Secondary English and Drama but didn't feel the time was right for me to teach. I hadn't felt the course had given me lots of confidence to teach either. Or maybe that was just me having to choose the direction for the next stage in my life, without feeling any sense of real direction or purpose other people seemed to have.

At home, now that we had all finished our education, mum was about to embark on her next adventure. She wanted to move. It seems this was something she had been planning for some time, something she had thought about, researched, and planned. She was about to make life easier for us all, while at the same time make our lives a lot more difficult to manage. She now had a focus on herself. This was clearly good for her mentally as she wanted to take her independence, and that gave her a positive focus. We couldn't tell or see if this was some sort of delusion. How do you know if someone's delusions are set to harm, or set to protect? Some people with paranoia will happily share their thoughts and beliefs, others not. Though still very difficult, you could know how their minds were working. But mum never shared in such a way. We never knew what was going on in her head. But we did know that it hadn't all gone away, and on that score, experience was going to prove us right every time. Whichever way you looked at it, we would always have to be looking out for her. She was perhaps in a more stable frame of mind to be able to plan in the way she had. But that did not mean life was going to get any easier, not for very long anyway.

CHAPTER 14

FAULTY MECHANICS

I found myself living with dad a while after college, an odd experience that no child really wants to go back to having tasted freedom. So it wasn't long before I was looking for somewhere to live. An old friend and neighbour had been renting a house locally and was about to leave, so I took it on. It was cheap, but there was good reason for that. It was a 1930s dump.

    I'd heard that one of my old secondary school teachers, Floss again as it happens, was moving and had to get rid of his piano. I had always enjoyed any music I was involved in and wanted to learn more myself. I was allowed some trumpet lessons at school, but never any support. I liked the idea of having a piano to maybe teach myself a little. At home my sister had the focus of music in her education at school and clearly showed some talent. And so she benefited from music lessons on piano and flute and could sing, managing grade eight in both. When it came to further education studying music and becoming a professional musician was an option for her. I always thought it a shame she went for the sensible choice and took a normal job when she clearly had that talent. But I guess working as a musician can be a difficult and insecure choice too.

The piano on offer to me was a boudoir grand. A little bigger than a baby grand. Not quite sure how I moved it now, but I do remember pushing it down the road on its side on a piano trolley for quite a while. I must've had help to travel it and manhandle it into the front room, where it dominated! It was a big thing to take on and move considering it was going into a rental property and might have to be moved again within the year, but I pledged to myself I would practice on it every day. I didn't have too much else on my agenda at that time after all.

I wasn't working, so was claiming benefits, felt despondent and very low. I guess I had come to the end of college and was stepping into quicksand. Three years of structure and now . . . a void. I had used those educational structures to support myself without thinking that I needed a plan, a dream, or a goal for myself. This is where I was realising that the wind had been taken out of my sails when I was younger, and I could see where it was beginning to have its impact. I had little money for winter heating. I can remember having a phone call with mum trying to explain that to her. Even now a conversation didn't really seem to connect with reality, though we exchanged words. I hadn't intended the conversation to go the way it did. I was trying to explain my situation to her, and I felt she wasn't understanding me. I wasn't on the scrounge for money, I just wanted her to appreciate I was having a hard time and I was feeling it. She seemed, as always to be somewhere else, on another planet, as if it didn't mean anything to her and it was nothing to do with her. I guess it wasn't. But there was no empathy or understanding. I put the phone down in frustration. And so, I was astonished to receive in the post a few days later, a cheque for two hundred pounds. All that energy I had put into our conversation had got through. Not because she sent me some money, but that I had made a connection with her for that moment about what was happening to me, and she had responded. She had at least understood my need if nothing else. God knows it took some work, but the prize was huge

It became a thing for a while that my brother would invite me over to his for Sunday roast in the evening. I was low, depressed and not much company. I didn't know what I was going to do next. One of the ways this helped was to force me to try and engage with life, with people again. Reluctant as you are when feeling down, the contact pushed me to re-engage, try and get things moving again. And it was my brother's way of helping. We talked about work a bit, but I had no direction to go in, my confidence was low and I wasn't in a frame of mind to go there anyway. Harping back to previous years, when I had no help or support, or direction. History didn't give me any security to fall back on.

Eventually things turned round. I don't know how or why, but life seemed to get busier. And much as I appreciated my brother's support, and especially his wife's excellent cooking, I didn't want to be there. I wanted to be getting on on my own.

It wasn't until my mid-twenties that I came to realise a name could be put to mum's illness. Up until then we all just knew she was mentally ill, but with no idea there was anything we could identify it with more specifically. That was just the way we had evolved and managed it as time developed. She would've then been in her late fifties. Of course, a diagnosis could also mean some sort of treatment, even perhaps a cure! When a problem is constant and draws on your energy, you never give up when it's your mother, even though you never really have her as a person, you still never give up.

Schizophrenia.

My brother and sister and I were beginning to home in on Schizophrenia as a sort of diagnosis. There were multiple symptoms of schizophrenia, and many key ones could be identified in my mum's behaviour. I researched and found a National Schizophrenic Fellowship group locally that met once a week, and I was there. Even in these times the awareness of mental illness to be able to identify a person's behaviour was unusual. There were no open conversations between people, families, where such specific information was available unless you had reason to search yourselves. Only then did groups such as the NSF show themselves. And that first meeting I attended was amazing. The first conversations I had were with parents, who mostly had children with some form of schizophrenia. But then there was one woman, just one, Judy, who identified closest with me with a parent and a brother suffering. As you might imagine, just to have someone understand what you are taking about, the same language and your experiences was just incredible. For the first time! The first time ever!

It was never my intention to put my mum in a box, but she was definitely in the frog room and fitted into a few of those boxes! It didn't matter which one, just that it was a means of understanding, so we could get some help for her, and perhaps some relief and maybe happiness.

All types of mental illness can be confused together or be happening at the same time. Depression is clearly major in itself, but also frequently a part of other mental illnesses. This wasn't a diagnosis, but it was a point of identification that was critical for me. Something I could try and understand. We knew only too well what her behaviour was. When you are not physically well, it's easy to tell the doctor what your symptoms are. And when the doctor tells you what the problem is and can offer some remedy you feel safe and confident and cared for. You'll get better.

We were all adults before we had at last got to first base. Identification meant we could talk about it with more accuracy. But the same problems were still there to get her to see anybody and get any sort of diagnosis or treatment if that was possible. At least, if we did talk to a professional, we could, with a word, describe the ballpark we thought we were in with a name!

In some respects that almost gave us more of a problem. With mental illness, nobody is readily willing to diagnose in detail. It is safer to retreat and give a general opinion, which you can't be held to. That's how it felt.

Consent was still the sticking point, and consent was what we didn't have.

CHAPTER 15

MILTON KEYNES

My mother had decided she wanted to move to Milton Keynes. Then a relatively new town with lots of new building still going on. It had long been a hobby of hers to take my dad out, taxi around and look at houses. I used to think it must be more of a hobby as I didn't otherwise know the reason. She could see a wonky line from a hundred paces and was always aware of possible bomb damage. Something which was a legitimate issue in the post war period. Though we were way past that. But I don't think any of us really understood why she had decided she wanted to move to Milton Keynes, apart from it would be a new house

As I, the last child, had finished my formal education, she decided the time was right for her to choose what she wanted to do. And that was to move to a new build in Milton Keynes. It's hard to understand the reasons behind her thinking, but it seemed to me she thought she might be able to give herself a new start by being on her own. She had lost the desire or need to be a part of the family. She wanted to be independent, on her own. Perhaps she thought that would be the happiest place for her. Perhaps she was taking herself away from everybody to protect us. Even with all the problems we had, my dad wasn't in favour. And though things were obviously not as they should be, and she had put him through a lot of stress, my dad had always provided that secure home for her in whatever circumstances. But she was insistent and so, with his eventual agreement and reluctant consent, she moved. Dad had done well in his work and was financially stable enough to enable the process. Mum hadn't had a job since the war years, but was claiming her part in the finances. She moved herself over an hour away from the rest of the family, who in some shape or form or combination would still have to look out for her.

Before she moved, she made an effort to sort her bad teeth out. She was clearly having a rejuvenation period. It wasn't just a case of popping down to the local dentist for her to sort them out. She decided she wanted to go to Harley Street and have a full job done. The works. And that was also the size of the project. I guess she felt she deserved it and they had the funds to make several trips up to London. And that is what she did. Within a number of months she had a new set of very valuable sparkling pearly whites! Two complete rows of crowns I believe. I can't imagine any tooth was worth keeping in its blackened rotting state.

It sounds like all was on the mend, those difficult times seemed as if they might be behind us. She was apparently turning full circle and engaging with normal life albeit very independently. Plans just for herself. And conversations were not open and free from other things still in her mind. But sadly, that engagement was not to last, and the clouds of troubled times were only occasionally broken with those bursts of sunshine. The storms were always going to return.

Hearing voices or other sounds is the most common hallucination.

- *female or male,*

- *someone you know or someone you've never heard,*
- *sounds such as humming,*
- *in a different language or different accent to your own,*
- *whispering or shouting, or*
- *negative and disturbing.*

Rethink Mental Illness

The new house was nice but mum wanted to make her mark and the garden especially needed work. She was different now, but far from well and still paranoid and hearing voices. My brother and I went up to build fences for her as it was a new plot. Concrete posts the lot. I went up a bit later and laid a path with very heavy concrete slabs, and a shed base. I was knackered. If I remember mum and I fell out at one point, as she had no idea of the weight of the job and didn't feel any acknowledgement for the work I was putting in. But it got done, and she spent many hours over the next few years sifting most of the soil for stones and rubble in about a sixty-foot garden and adding lots of fertilizer, laying more slabs and planting many flowers.

She wasn't lonely, but it was hard to know where she was in her head living alone and apparently isolated. Now I look back at this time, the simple but serious and effective work of making her garden beautiful was massive therapy for her in the summer months and took a huge amount of her time. Ironically, it would be her family who would visit and tell her how lovely it looked and what a good job she was doing. She quite normally but ironically wanted some recognition for that work.

In Isobel Hardman's book *The Natural Health Service* she talks and delves deeply into the potential benefits of being outside and with nature. How it has been proven to be hugely beneficial for mental balance and health for anyone. Each of us has our own scenario for which the choices we make work for us best. From being able to see trees outside your hospital window to being out amongst the wonderful natural world we often take for granted. Isobel herself talks a lot about how elements of it were her saviour and absorption a saving grace. So logical to me now. If the choice, particularly for our youth, is of flashing busy bright screens constantly designed to get your attention and taking you down mostly unsatisfactory paths, against absorbing a stunning natural environment with incredible beauty, interest and detail which we are naturally grounded with. It's blindingly obvious which will stress, and which will soothe. And that's just the tip of the iceberg albeit a melting one.

It is significant that mum took the decision to move away and be on her own. She didn't worry about being lonely or having company. She didn't strive to meet people or make new friends, belong to any groups or clubs. She was already isolated and on her own wherever she was. She had the company of herself, and in mum's case, there was more going on than any of us would welcome. That existence she had in her mind was her life, and in a way all the company that absorbed her. Having a simple job of sorting the garden, which was hard work, was what she used for occupation, the therapy and connection with nature which filled her mind. Later in her life it would simplify to colouring in children's books. This time purely to occupy her mind, though not always completely successful.

A while after she moved in, we became aware of mum's deterioration again. Curtains were closed and behaviour more introverted. My brother booked a local GP to visit. We decided we would not tell mum. We knew she would not co-operate. We would not tell the doctor, because he would refuse to visit without the patient's consent, but we would arrive just before him so we could explain to mum what we had done and could then let him in. Honesty, but not till the last moment. It was the only way to stand a chance of achieving some success.

We arrived together, which caused my mum a little concern, though she was clearly not in the best state to challenge us. That fiery and robust person mum had been was now much depleted. We explained that the doctor was due in a few minutes. When he arrived, we invited him in and explained what we had done, the situation and our concerns. He wasn't best pleased but thankfully was prepared to listen. Apart from my mum's haggled appearance and worried state, she had laid us out a gem to work with. At previous events she was far too clever to be able to catch her out. There would always be an answer, but not only that, one that would fit in with perceived normal behaviour. In other words, an unsuspecting person would have no reason to think anything untoward. This was different. She was as she believed in her frailty though she almost seemed aware she was giving the game away. She was tormented by her state of mind. To explain to the doctor, she told him the messages were to do with the heating. The radiators were hot upstairs, but cold down. She invited him to check and so give him an understanding of what was happening. To mum that was a critical message and gave that away to the GP. The closed curtains were to protect her from more messages. If she couldn't see out, she couldn't read any messages.

Truth was the central heating pump had broken, so the heat rose, as it does, and could only heat the upstairs radiators. No pump to get the heat around the system and downstairs. My mum would not even contemplate this might be the reason. The doctor was kind and understanding, but again unless my mum asked for help herself, there was nothing he could do. We left feeling we had achieved something. But to little avail. We were still gradually but properly understanding just how difficult it was to get help without mum's consent. Only if she became a danger to herself or others could this be achieved. It was a number of years later sadly before we were to reach this stage.

When she had been in Milton Keynes a while, I decided I had to try and switch off from her and focus onto what I was doing. I had to try and think about me. I was naturally trained for her to always have a space in my mind and be a concern. But I had to address that for my own sake. Events in fact would always bring that back.

It was around this time my partner was concerned that I was worrying about mum a lot, and suggested that I might get some counselling to help with the issue. Having someone look out for me with love and support in motherly matters was a lovely feeling. It still wasn't a subject I would talk about to most people, but of course couldn't be ignored in a relationship. I saw a counsellor she knew. I was a little cautious but willing.

I think I must've had at least half a dozen sessions, maybe more. I found it interesting, but it was a new idea for me to share so much of my experiences with another and found the terms of counselling quite difficult to get used to. His ultimate conclusion was that I had had a 'bleak childhood'. I'm not sure how I felt about that at the time. Some recognition and confirmation of the problems of course, but when it is your own experience, you never see it quite like that, and I didn't feel as if I had talked to him with that in mind.

And as for my worries about mum and the reason for seeing a counsellor in the first place, I think I knew all along that my concerns were just a reality. At times I inevitably worried about her, her state, and how we were all going to manage her. That was just a fact. If it were a family member who had cancer or some other serious illness, we would all have them in our minds. From this perspective mental illness is no different. And it continues, because in all those scenarios, the care can be long and the patient doesn't always get better.

This was the time for me to focus more on what I wanted to do. It had always been in my mind to go travelling at some point and now was a good time. Having worked at Richmond Theatre after college and toured around the country as an Assistant Stage Manager for over a year I had decided it was time to go. My brother was now working in Hong Kong and an old school friend had emigrated to Australia. The framework was there. The final catalyst was an Inland Revenue rebate into my account. A rare event and clearly a sign that I should get a move on. And so plans turned into actions. I was on my way.

CHAPTER 16

THE DROP IN DOWN UNDER

I had been in Australia on my travels for best part of a year. I flew from my brother's home in Hong Kong from where I had already been to the Philippines, Macau, and a day trip into China. From Hong Kong, I flew on to Perth via Malaysia and Singapore. The Perth flight was the cheapest one to Australia, and I was on a budget. I had to eventually get myself to Sydney. But first found a variety of jobs in Perth to keep me going. I rolled newspapers early in the morning, bit of an Aussie thing, mopped carpets in a hospital by day, bit of a crazy thing, and worked in a music hall in the evening. But before I could pick up all these jobs, funds were getting a bit tight for paying my $12 rent per week for my room in a shared house.

    I was lucky as I met another Brit on the flight across, who was joining his Aussie girlfriend in Perth.

There was a room in their house going, so I jumped at the offer. For some reason it didn't bother me being low on funds. I know I was in a foreign country on the other side of the world, one where you had to prove you had funds in your bank before they would let you in. I guess I could always call home and ask for a loan. But that wasn't part of the plan. I know I was down to my last few Aussie dollars, but there was a lovely sense of freedom in being there and having no money. After all I was by the sea, the sun shone, and all was good. I had a wonderful sense of freedom.

  I eventually bought an old Holden HR car from one of my house mates. It seemed a good idea as it was registered in New South Wales, and that was where I was heading next, to Sydney. Across the Nullarbor and across Australia! Eventually. That meant I would be selling it in its home territory which was New South Wales. It had a decent three-litre engine, and when my housemate said she wanted to sell it, I thought that works for me.

As it was going to make a long drive across Australia of several thousand miles, I thought I'd take it up country to Geraldton for a few days to see how it went. Hoping nothing would go wrong and it wouldn't break down. It was a fair way, but all went well except I thought I needed to get the clutch checked. I can't remember why, though an Australian friend did notice something before I went but didn't say as he thought events should take their natural path for my long trip. Needless to say, he was a friend I felt I could've done without. The clutch plate was cracked, and replacement probably cost the cheap clutch place more than the job was worth, but thankfully luck was with me.

I sent my dad, a postcard saying I'm just about to drive across Australia. I'll send you a card when I get the other side. I thought nothing of it, but apparently that raised an eyebrow.

I spend the next few months driving 7000 miles across, up and around and down Australia with a three other mates I'd met in Perth, getting dehydrated, checking out opals at Cooper Pedy, drinking beer in the pool whilst observing Ayers Rock (now rightly renamed Uluru), trekking through The Olgas, sleeping out and cooking every night round the fire, picking mangoes, tomatoes, sleeping with snakes, though unaware, being left on the Whitsunday Islands for a week, and many more things in the outback. It was a drive to remember till suddenly as we drove south, after miles and miles of beautiful Australian yellows and burnt amber, we hit carpets of green grass and big chunky towns down the east coast.

I got to Sydney and found my old school friend who I was going to stay with. Having emigrated there with his family he and his girlfriend kindly put me up in their flat in Manley, north edge of Sydney Harbour, and surfing was the order of the day. He was a mad surfer. To be quite honest, he was a bit mad full stop. But I could not stay with my friend and his partner forever. Events took over, and my problem was . . . solved.

I didn't really know how mum was coping at this stage, but she had now decided that she wanted to travel and do things she never had the opportunity to do before in her life. Great! Good for her.

Why am I saying that - there is always a consequence . . .

My dad never wanted to leave the UK for holidays, so mum felt now was her chance. She had arranged to visit my brother in Hong Kong, and I, ever the optimist, invited her over to Oz. Just a hop and a skip further. I think we were both playing the optimist.

Never an easy person to deal with, my mother arrived in Hong Kong, and before long relations were strained. A lot of the problem seemed to be that she had no concept of jet lag. She had just flown many hours and changed time zones but did not have the awareness in any way that this would require some adjustment and time to recoup. Or even that it had happened! A jet lag time bomb.

And so, I received the message that she refused to stay in Hong Kong another night, having I think only stayed there for one and she was on her way to Sydney with the extra caveat of 'sorry she is not in the best state'.

I appreciated the warning and waited at the airport to meet her, not quite knowing what to expect. Her flight was still a significant duration to Sydney, without having adjusted to the first one, so I was getting double bubble. Eventually she appeared. She nearly always had a worried and preoccupied look about her, but that was a slither of what I was about to greet.

There appeared an angry tight lipped, fraught, worried and strained face, her hair wild and frizzy almost as if she'd had her head out of the cockpit for the whole journey. Oh dear. What, why had I done it? The next few weeks were going to be . . . challenging.

Strangely we never seemed to shield ourselves from getting involved in what might be for other people, more normal activities. We didn't try to prevent her from doing what she wanted, though that would've been fruitless anyway, but tried to look after her when we could. The idea of my mum being capable of travelling the world solo was frankly absurd. But here we were, on the other side of the world. Optimism always prevailing. One down and one to go.

Luckily, I was able to rent a small flat in the block I was already in for us both, so we had somewhere to stay, and by the beach. But mum didn't live a normal life. She wasn't in her own safe environment, with familiar surroundings, and things she might potter with or British TV to watch. I remember her sitting with nothing to do and again, not realising the jet lag, and being in a strange place. My brothers flat in Honk Kong was his home and in the place he worked. There were all the home comforts. I was travelling and basically living a more mobile life. Perfect for me, hopeless for her without the normal ability to live. But we tried. I'd give it about a 50/50. We went to see the QE2 come into harbour in Sydney, visited a few places and I guess I tried to be tour operator to a child who could do little for herself.

She had made herself a swimsuit bikini type of thing at home and brought it with her. Something suitable for a woman knocking sixty. She wouldn't have had anything like that otherwise unless she made it for herself. So, in her mind she was planning a project and an adventure. She just didn't have the ability to live it out. She didn't understand that, but in her naivety it wasn't going to stop her trying. We walked to the beach nearby at Manley, and she paddled in the shallow waters in her newly made bikini. It didn't occur to me she wouldn't be able to manage herself there. But I hadn't been on a beach with her since . . . well not in my memory, and I would've been the child.

She was still in the shallows in her bikini when a wave came along and knocked her over. It wasn't in her mind to be prepared. She was a child. Not even with the basic instincts to manage her environment. It knocked her over and under the water momentarily and she chocked a little on some of the sea water. It was my fault she cried because I hadn't 'warned her to close her mouth'. I had to be more than a parent. She was upset and it properly hit home I was looking after my child like mum. She was out of her comfort zone, and I was the responsible adult. The biggest part of that problem was that she had no grasp or awareness of it. But then if that was her state, why would she be aware any more than a child would be.

    She settled after a while, and we visited some sights. But I was pleased and relieved when I finally had my freedom back, and she was safely on a plane back home. How we came to the decision it was time to go and we had to book a flight I don't know. Of course, no Internet then. But it must have been amicable. I don't remember how long she visited. At least a couple of weeks. I am constantly amazed at my optimistic naivety in expecting such events with my mother to be perhaps making some happy memories together, something to look back on and reminisce about. The fun times and experiences we had together. But it is always about managing and making the best of often difficult circumstances.

When she got back home she would be able to readjust to her own familiar environment. I wonder how she reflected on her experience. I have no idea.

Me, I was ready to carry on with my trip home before my visa ran out, via India and Nepal, go to an old girlfriend's wedding in Delhi and back home in time for my sister's wedding. One my mother sadly would choose not to attend. Everyone here has their story.

CHAPTER 17

SUTTON

My mother had been in Milton Keynes several years and her state of mind was getting no better. Her back garden was immaculate. Hours, days, months, years of hard work to occupy her and make it a very well managed beautiful garden. But she was still a long way away to manage and she was getting no younger either.

My brother was living in a close in Sutton, and one of the houses on the other side of the close became available. It was decided the time right to try move her back more locally. It was clear life wasn't going to get any easier, and we would have to keep a close eye on her. Her more placid yet still trying state was such that the move looked like it would be easier than we could have hoped. There wasn't the fight in her we might have once had, although she still had it and she had to agree obviously, or none of this could be done. There perhaps wasn't the desire to be so independent anymore, but consent . . . after all, again. There were nail biting moments. If I thought my mum knew I would've said she had us on the edges of our seats many a time. In a way, I sort of think she did, and this was her only mechanism to protect herself. Sadly, everyone was under suspicion, as had been for very many years. When you are tormented, there is no safe haven. Everyone is guilty.

Somehow, we managed to get her moved and squeezed into a two-bedroom terrace in Sutton. She settled relatively well in her new home. She had passed that active stage and the garden was no longer of such interest to her but sitting a lot and watching TV was. A bit loud for some of the terraced neighbours, but ok. She had always been a bit deaf in one ear, increasing with age. We always thought that was likely another consequence of her meningitis.

I would occasionally take my dad over to visit his sister who lived in Bexleyheath. There had been many years previously, I assume, where their relationship was by phone alone. She was always very grateful because otherwise she would never see him. I don't recall any of his sisters had learnt to drive in those days. As I mentioned earlier with mum's sensitivities, there were always times when some sisters would have fallen out with others. Even in their more mature years their differences were still evident.

I was now engaged to be married and driving with my aunt one day, just the two of us in the car when she said to me. 'I wondered if you would ever get married'. She was referring to mum and clearly thought that the damage done to me by the effect of mum's mental health would be enough to make me incapable of a relationship which would lead to marriage. It shocked me as I didn't see myself as so handicapped. I didn't think I was. But then I had no idea of the conversations my dad had with her over the years. And as I wasn't included, they had no idea where I was either. Perhaps it was a realisation on her part that I might be as capable and normal as anyone else. After all, many people have challenging scenarios in their lives and manage them positively. I guess you would have to ask others how deluded I might have been.

At thirty four I got married and some years later my three young children enjoyed the attention my aunt gave them. She was one of two of my aunts we had contact with now. The other lived in Wells, where we visited a couple of times for their big carnival in November. The only family we occasionally connected with as she had three children, my cousins, of similar ages to my brother sister and me. Dad had kept up once secret phone calls, usually on a Sunday evening I think, to many of his sisters and brother. But rarely saw any of them. In fact, a few times he did see them I drove him.

Now settled in Sutton mum was back in the mode of doing things for herself again. She had bad bunions, something quite common in that generation as they often wore ill-fitting shoes in their youth. Mum's big toes were heading east and west instead of north, and walking was painful, so she decided to have them operated on and fixed.

Times must've been more settled again. Once home after the operation I made her a loose pair of slippers from old blackout material my dad still had around from the war, and some inner soles. With just a stapler and a pair of scissors I managed to construct a simple slipper to keep her sore feet warm whilst they healed. I remember this because I achieved some appreciation for doing it from mum. There weren't many simple opportunities to show any caring, but when they came up and were well received, they were very important to take.

The appreciation in this case was much more valuable as the thought for me. It was a reassurance that it was always worth making the effort, even if only the odd occasion hit the spot. The trail was pitch black, but those occasional markers proved that it was always the right one

My dad used to take mum shopping for her food supplies once a week but was finding the stress of it all too much. He still looked after her financial matters, but she was just a stress for him. Patient a man as he was, she obviously could persistently thump a sensitive spot in him he could not protect, and she hit his stress button constantly. He could not cope.

My sister and I mucked in. I took a long lunch from work when I could and took her instead. It was never an easy task and was certainly no fun. Testing the patience of a saint was a mild term. She lived on ready meals and lots of choc ices. Her shape changed to being much more rounded, and less mobile. My children used to laugh their socks off when Grandma would sit herself down on a now very depressed sofa at one end, her head hitting the back whilst her legs flew up in the air showing . . . well you can imagine . . . if she'd remembered.

We didn't visit too often when my children were small. Grandma had nothing to offer them. She used childrens' colouring in books to occupy herself and sooth her sense of anxiety a lot of the day, filling in the pictures with felt tip pens. We had to keep her well supplied which was at times a challenge. There would sometimes be a panic as we realised she was running out of books or felt pens and the right ones would not always be readily available. But, when we would visit with the children, mum couldn't understand why they would want to do some colouring too. They wouldn't understand why they couldn't. Naturally they would just sit at the table and colour. They thought it was for them! Only to be told off. Visits to Grandma weren't too popular, or common.

CHAPTER 18

BLESS THIS HOUSE

Mum was now sixty five and once she was settled in Sutton, I took the opportunity to contact the local Catholic Church, as they would visit people who had moved into the area to welcome them and perhaps bless the house.

Going back to the religious theory, this seemed an opportunity not to miss, and any opportunity was not to be missed. I told her I had been to see the local priest. The idea was met with no enthusiasm but the usual suspicion. I told her he would visit to say hello and offer to bless the house. He did visit, and sent me this letter afterwards:

Dear Greg

I did call on your mother last week and I'm afraid I did not have much success. I suggested that she might like the house blessed but she did not feel she wanted that to happen. She was very interested to know how I knew she was living there and I mentioned that I had met you, and as a result, I had suggested the blessing of the house.

After that rejection I later asked mum if she wanted to come with me to mass at the church. She said she did. It felt like there was a chink in her armour, an indication that she was at a weak stage and perhaps now allowing herself to look back to her religious connections. We sat near the back of the church, and it was clear her mind was buzzing, but she was quite frail and pathetic in her way. Who knows what was going through her mind, but it could only have been a positive thing. It came to Holy Communion towards the end of the service, and I thought I'd chance the question and asked her if she would like to go up. She just turned and looked at me with a sad face and her big solemn brown eyes and said, 'I haven't been to confession.' It was a rather pathetic look as if to ask what she should do. She gave the impression of being completely helpless, and perhaps even guilty at her lack of engagement with her religion before. I said I was sure it wouldn't matter.

'I'll take you up,' I said, and she took my arm. We walked slowly up to the altar.

Tradition had changed and helpfully you could now stand rather than kneel as the priest came along the line, and mum took Holy Communion.

On whatever level that happened for her, I cannot imagine how she felt on that day. At the very least she had connected again with something she had apparently discarded. Either because she felt rejected, or she felt unworthy. It was many years since she went to her local church in Tolworth and asked for help from her faith. She was told to take a holiday. That uncaring and abrupt, but not surprising response of the time meant she had apparently turned her back on the Church for all those years where it may well have been a positive influence. I cannot say that with any confidence though, as her illness kept all and everybody at arm's length. Perhaps this just happened to be a moment when it came together for her. Perhaps now she felt some solace in her religion again. Initially she rejected her religion, but in fact ultimately, she only rejected the messenger

Catholicism gave you a conscience, she always used to complain. She didn't want her faith to make her feel guilty. It was something she valued and ultimately meant much more to her than a judgement.

CHAPTER 19

SIT DOWN AND CHAT

Mum could hit everybody's stress button. It is the nature of this mental illness, particularly one such as schizophrenia, where, to them, their world and any way of living with it is the real one, and they are quite able to argue that point to the very end. There is no way around that as it is absolute. You will not ever get through with any other idea however correct or real it is. What I didn't realise for many years growing up, is that maybe because it was my mum, I would always naturally approach her from my norm, because it is of course where we all start from. No matter how that is received, we will always start from where we are. Our reality. So, every time I would try to communicate with my mum, however simple, I was always knocked back.

I was holding on to my own sanity. It isn't something I registered at the time, but I would feel the consequence. Because as soon as you enter any interaction, you are stepping over a battle line from which you can never win. That absorbs energy, mind space, and leaves you unable to communicate in a normal relaxed way. It's a constant state of dissatisfaction and frustration. It leaves you with no place to be settled, relaxed, comfortable with that person. Settled, relaxed, comfortable with yourself. It's a type of constant agitation of not being able to fulfil a simple human activity. And because it was my mother, it was one I instinctively expected to fulfil. But never could. So, much as behaviours, incidents, arguments all took their toll in our lives and what I coped with and managed, I could never get to communicate with my mum. Because she was, at the most basic level, not there.

Whilst she was living in Sutton, I decided I should try something. I sat opposite my mum and tried to talk directly to her about the whole situation. I had to bang my head against the wall. Even after what I have just said, it was something I felt I had to try. And I was prepared for whatever response I might get. Maybe looking her in the eye facing everything head on and calmly discussing what was happening might illicit some normal reaction.

Thinking about it after the event, that was so wishful I know. It did get a sort of response, but in completely the wrong context. When I said my piece, stopped and looked at her, waiting for some response, she looked back at me and smiled, almost laughed at me as you might to a young child who had tried hard but misunderstood something. She didn't attempt to engage in any way.

I almost felt as if I had broken through, because she listened, and didn't actively react. Almost an appreciation of the effort. But I hadn't. I was the one guilty of delusion. The smile I felt was one of humouring me. A pat on the back for maybe caring a little, trying but no cigar.

At another event around the same time, whilst we were 'having words', she surprised me and said, 'I love all you children you know.' Something I only ever heard her say once, and my father never.

When my children were young my wife had to remind me to tell my children that I loved them. It was an action or words that I just wasn't used to saying.

Not because I didn't love them of course. The most precious love I have is for my children. But because it was never said to me. It wasn't a part of normal behaviour or speak in my life. And it wasn't just the words I wasn't used to; it was opening up those feelings and emotions that went with the words. Openly expressing that love.

As a society we are much more open with our emotional expressiveness for the most part in the 2020s. That in itself helps someone with my experiences break down those barriers. Because it isn't just a case of getting use to saying the words. It carries what I lost for never hearing them myself, or actions which backed them up, and how important that would've been.

These experiences on their own, or lack of them would be easier to manage. But when you put them into the big dysfunctional picture, the numbness and ultimate confusion, lack of a concrete anchor and direction when home life is never a complete thing, understanding someone coming from that background perhaps becomes clearer.

Perhaps it is important now to stress my mother never had any hatred or malice for any of us. Frustration of course as I had with my retaliation to her on many an occasion, but never hatred. Her head was her own and upset, anger, and frustration were all directed out to wherever or whatever was going on in her world. Never intentionally to us.

CHAPTER 20

CHAMELEON

I have already talked about having groups of friends where I am one of three and usually the outsider. The more I have thought about this the more I realise that as I grew up, I had unwittingly acquired a skill. I was encouraging people to think that I was more in the thick of events, or sometimes relationships than I actually was. I could create a space whereby I could be in touch with what was going on, but not involved in the hub of it all. I was trying to be a part of life around me but my story was preventing me doing it in a normal way.

I'm reluctant to identify myself as an outsider because that was precisely what I was trying to avoid. I wanted to be a part of everything as best I could, knowing that my family life was alien to everybody else's. And what I was doing was normality for me. That was the best I could do. I accepted that and I knew no better. Maybe everybody did that in their own way. Probably some might have for their own reasons or problems.

I naturally evolved this ability because I knew my home experience was so different to everyone else's. Something I instinctively knew, but I couldn't communicate why to anybody. Mostly because there was nobody to exercise those thoughts and feelings with, and people I would relate to out of my home wouldn't have a clue what I was talking about. They had communication, relationships with their families, uncles, aunts, grandparents, cousins, family friends, people who they could talk to. People who would want to talk to them and make sure they were ok.

In a normal family environment, we use the feedback we get from our family, friends, to use in how we interact with those around us, to conform or rebel. We use feedback to give us an anchor to work from, and a position of reference to be able to move on from. It allows us a learning process, to develop. It is a structural loss in that development of a child not to have parents, elders and peers in your family to complete that picture. The more I write about this consequence the more I realise just how pivotal and critical an element of growing up family and friends are, and how hard it is to imagine growing up without that structure.

Though I partially knew these differences, this wasn't the time I would realise just what effect that would have. I needed some reference to understand. Yes, I already felt different, but I was developing my own skills instinctively to cope with this.

As a young adult I could leave that behind me as I went out into the world to tread my own path. My background I couldn't deny, but I could then see for the first time just how different that had made me, the things I had missed, the way I was, the way I worked. In a way it was a shock, and gradually as things dawned on me over quite a long period of time, I realised how much I had to do to find myself a stable base to work from.

I suppose this was when my own life was beginning.

How did I feel about that?

What skills and understanding did I have?

How would I react to fitting myself in with my own identity?

All the trials and tribulations of family life would all still be with me and frequently return, as none had really been resolved or gone away, but I would gradually be able to separate how I moved forward. And that was true.

Or was it?

When you are managing a problem, which effects the fundamentals of your development, that problem drains away from your energy to pursue your own objectives. We all have our strengths and weakness whether they be as simple as academic or practical. You may be a top chef but be rubbish at maths. Be a highflyer in the city, but barely able to change a light bulb. But those are standard everyday capabilities. Aside of examples like those, imagine if you do have abilities but your mind is busy coping with what life is throwing at you, where you stand, draining your energy to focus on yourself and what you might be capable of. Not just a distraction but actually sapping that fuel which gives you direction, strength and foresight to make the best of yourself. Most people wouldn't even consider these issues in their lives as we all take certain things for granted. And that is so good because people can focus on bigger and better futures in whichever way they might go.

But if you are coping with somebody, especially a close family member, especially your mum with severe mental illness, who is pivotal in giving you so much in your life, that path to achieve ceases to be clear and available. Rather than a sharp focus it becomes a flat pancake.

I was probably developing more of an understanding than a freedom. In a way I had developed skills and understanding to manage my situation others didn't have. I was more aware and perceptive, though I did not always feel that was to my advantage.
Something there couldn't be changed or ignored.

CHAPTER 21

FOUND OUT

Out of the blue, one cold frosty mid-winter night, we had a call from the local police to say my mother had been found walking around Sutton some three quarters of a mile or more away from her home, with no coat on. She was worried and confused. They somehow managed to find out where she lived and took her home again, to find all the lights on and her front door wide open.

CHAPTER 22

SECTION

Over time, mum had gone full circle and we were aware she had lost weight. As my brother, sister and I investigated, we discovered she was being 'told' that her food was poisoned, and so she couldn't – wouldn't eat anything. Between my brother , sister and I we began to think of ways we'd be able to get her eating again. Dad had taken more of a back seat by this time, finding it much harder to manage her. She had lost a lot of weight and had become very frail. We made sure she had food and arranged to take her out to lunch between us amongst other things, but by now she was getting very thin. Her face was so lean she had a skeletal look. Her features were giving way to her bone structure. People were inevitably looking at her and staring. It was a frightening look which made any onlooker wonder why somebody might be so thin. Maybe some physical illness, a cancer, or just very old age, but nobody would think this woman is so thin because she had been told her food had been poisoned and she couldn't eat it. What other people were seeing meant nothing to my mum, but it was disturbing to see. The system of 'can't do anything unless she asks' was becoming increasingly problematic, but until a critical situation was to occur, the system were sitting on their hands. Much as we tried, they weren't going to move voluntarily. Consent was becoming stretched to its limits and we needed to press and get some action. If we didn't the road we were treading was obvious. Only an emergency would provoke a reaction. She was now around five and a half stone. So, what constitutes an emergency? Was it 'the present' and the condition she was in, the inevitable consequence of that, or was it the eventual 'outcome' of that state, which would clearly be too late. Too late meaning she wouldn't survive. Conversations had with the 'system' were not producing results, so we decided on a course of action. My brother put together a letter, which would bring both those positions together in a way we hoped they couldn't ignore. It meant laying out the situation as stark as it was, but also making it clear of the consequences should no action be taken. And that critical element was to say we would hold them accountable for not taking the necessary action to look after mum. There was only one option. They needed to agree to assess and Section her.

Thankfully, this had the desired effect and arrangements were made to meet at her house. Three professionals were required for such an event. A doctor, a social worker, and a psychiatrist, or psychiatric nurse, if I remember correctly. It may be different now. One of us had to be there to let everybody in. As we each had our strengths in managing events and processes that would be thrown at us, this was one I felt I could do and manage.

I arrived at the house before the designated time to be sure I could get in and be able to let everyone else in. Not surprisingly my mum wouldn't let me through the door. She was very frail, weak and confused, and was being very nice to me, but I wasn't the good guy, and she wasn't going to let me in. My only option was to go around the back of the terrace and break in through the kitchen window. She was in no state to stop me, even work out what was happening, and if the neighbours called the police, well then, we'd have got more than we bargained for. I accessed around the back and went to the kitchen window. I called to try and persuade mum to open a window just in case, but I was wishful, and had to smash a small window, open the bigger one and climb in, trying not to upset or alarm her. In truth much could've happened around her this evening, and I doubt she would have had the capacity to take any of it in, let alone react. Such was her frail state.

It wasn't long before the professionals arrived, and we all sat down quite calmy to assess the situation. Once I heard the words that she was in such a state she needed to be sectioned, I sighed in relief. The object of many days concern work and worry by us all had been realised. The assessment took place, she was sectioned and calmly taken into a psychiatric hospital.

A milestone in her history. In our family history. Now well in her sixties this was the first time, the very first time after all the years of distress and torment she'd had, she was finally going to get some sort of care and diagnosis. It took her to be at deaths door before it could happen.

We all felt drained and relieved in a way that now her care was in someone else's hands, and not just ours. It would be understood, diagnosed, and hopefully treated.

But it was another situation each of us felt differently about. Even after all the troubles with mum, there was always a feeling, for some more than others, of it not being right letting someone else take the responsibility. A bit like should you put your parents into a home. But we did agree here that we had reached the limit, and much as nobody wants to section their own mother, there was no other responsible way to look after and protect her.

She was cared for in hospital for three months on medication and was quickly becoming institutionalised. Understandably there were all sorts of people with all kinds of mental illness around her, and worryingly mum seemed a bit at home, but maybe she just didn't take in most of those people. Her world was quite insular. She was happy to be looked after and in company. Ironically everything through her life she had eventually pushed away for an isolated life and frame of mind.

CHAPTER 23

HOSPITAL VISITS

We tried to make sure one of us could visit Mum every day while she was in hospital. She was put on medication of course and began to eat again. As time went on, she seemed content, and although a lot of the company around her was quite 'extrovert', it didn't seem to bother her. But then that's my view. Why would she be bothered? It was company for her, which maybe was beneficial. She would otherwise never choose company, but whilst she had no choice, she was happy to be part of the hospital community to the point that she was becoming institutionalised.

When it came to diagnosis, well then it becomes complicated. This is when doctors are cautious, non-committal, and frustrating. That sounds like a criticism, but mental illness is such a collection of different problems often overlapping in their symptoms. But in truth there were limits as to what they could diagnose from what they see in front of them as opposed to the long history we related. We of course laid out as much of her history as we could. Having explained everything we could think of. The doctors came back with, if my memory serves me correctly, senile schizophrenia. I may have not got that completely right, but it doesn't matter. It was the medical snapshot of what they could see at that time, and totally frustrating to us with the decades of knowledge and experience we had, but a lesson learnt about getting expectations up in such a situation. I could still remember years before going to that first meeting of the National Schizophrenic Fellowship and feeling the relief in identifying what was troubling my mum.

After three months she went home on medication to stop the voices. And probably more.

My mum was always a physically sensitive person. Her skin was always sensitive to strong chemical-based bio washing powders and suchlike, and she was sensitive to medications too. Consequently, once she had settled back home and realised her situation, she gradually reduced her medication until she was off it altogether. This took a while, but eventually there seemed no consequence from the action. The voices did not apparently re appear.

That we were aware.

CHAPTER 24

SAD 1

There have been three events in my life which I have always remembered as my saddest moments.

This was the first of these.

Since the time my mum had initially shown signs of suffering from mental illness, and my desire for it all to go away to be able to see who my real mum was, there needed an event like this for me to realise:

My mother was never going to get better.

She was never going to be normal.

Especially she was never going to be normal.

I was never going to have a normal mum.

I now realise that the person I was losing at the beginning of this story when I was eight years old had properly gone away, which even at that age gave me cause for some grief of that loss. Understanding and support, particularly from the larger family, has been shown to be very effective in managing loss. But that had long been dismantled. It has also been shown that being reminded and reassured of how mum used to be when normal could also have been a big help in managing that loss. Then there is the grief which leaves you with the constant reminder of loss as that person is still around, but the loss of past and future expectations still remain. You can mourn the loss of the person, and the part they haven't and will never play.

It sounds crazy, but without realising, I always kept a small place in my mind, in my heart, that one day I might have a normal mum. You hold on to some hope. You do don't you. You always hold on to the tiniest bit of hope.

Until something happens that finally closes the door.

CHAPTER 25

RETURN

And so, life continued.

Less physically able, relatively stable mentally. In the time she was in hospital we cleaned up her house, but we had to make sure all was back in the exact place, because she would notice and change would upset her. That wasn't worth going through. We drew on my TV production experience and took continuity photos of everything, so it could all go back without a thing being out of place. Success, it went well

Don't be fooled though into a false sense of security. Mum was still a very difficult woman, and difficult to manage.

We couldn't just change her very sunken sofa, that was something that would ring alarm bells. It gave her a sense of security. As time progressed she was assessed at home and she had someone come in to help her with meals and other important things which she seemed to accept. Perhaps she was appreciating company again.

A little later she decided she needed a new armchair to sit in. She was now also doubly incontinent, and life was becoming more uncertain in other ways. I did a little research and offered to take her to look at, test and buy a new chair. Her feet weren't very good and walking distance wasn't easy, so it was worth a little planning. It was a full afternoon, and to tell my brother and sister how it went, I decided to write the event at the time as a short story.

CHAPTER 26

ADVENCHAIR

Mum's 'advenchair' sorted at last.

I decided, after talking to the chair company (nobody really knew what they were talking about) that I needed to take Mum to the shop to try one out.

I saw her on the Saturday, but it was her birthday, and I didn't want to take her then in case she had birthday visitors. That would only be us of course. So I went back on Sunday. I waited while she finished her lunch, and then found her a coat. She threw herself down on her now very low sofa, her head thumping on the back while her legs flew up in the air confirming to me, thankfully, that she was in fact wearing her pull ups. Then, true to fashion, she decided she didn't want to go.

After about ten minutes of me getting a bit shirty, or 'persuasive' with her, she decided, in her slippers and old coat, which she insisted was mine, to come. I ask you, me in a girlie coat!

She enjoyed the drive to Caterham with all the trees and cars, the like of which she hadn't seen for many months. Meanwhile, I was becoming aware of some poignant odours emitting from inside the car for which I was not responsible and was reassured that ladies didn't do such things. My suspicions were aroused.

We arrived at the shop. Mum's strenuous efforts to get out of the car on her own were foiled, mainly by the seat belt she had forgotten she was wearing. I levered her out and we hobbled into the store, where I plonked her down on the chosen chair on which she felt immediately at home.

'Ah bless', the lady said as she tried to remember where she had seen me before. Surprisingly it took more than a little memory jogging for her to remember it was the previous day in that same shop. My worry of course was that mum was going to crap on a nice new £700 display chair. A swift exit, should this occur, was clearly not a plan! The long coat she was wearing did cover as a little insurance against the act but not the embarrassment. Let's hope the pull ups could hold a potential onslaught.

'Ah bless' the sales assistant sighed over and over again as she tried her professional best to make somebody feel at ease. Probably herself.

I hoisted mum up to try another nearby chair, the smaller model, which she also liked but decided it was a little too cosy for her short but rotund bulk. The choice was tall and wide or short and narrow. Sadly, short and wide wasn't an option, so biggest and strongest was the choice.

I told her to stay sat while I did the deal. The catalogue I had showed cheaper prices as they had just increased, but the lady was happy to honour the price I had. At this point, Mum was on the move again. Having passed through her short memory cycle she had concluded, as the chair was facing the other way and couldn't see me, that I had abandoned her, and she was off to get herself into a panic. As she turned, she saw me. I told her to sit down and rest at which point she plonked back into the chair as if attached by a super strong piece of elastic. If I had previously any doubt about the height of the chair, I now felt confident that this sort of treatment was sure to take a good few inches off the cushion height by sheer force and compression. Things were looking good.

The sales assistant wrote everything out in long hand in amazingly neat detail, a demonstration of perhaps how boring her job really was. I helped the lady conclude the transaction by ensuring she had an address to deliver the chair to. A small detail, but one she had managed to overlook. £713 later, the standard chair being £13 more expensive than the one I had earmarked, and the option of £30 for stain treatment, pull ups or no pull ups, was a must. That makes me £43 out of pocket. Mum contained herself and the sales assistant didn't have to say 'Ah bless' yet again.

We stumbled back to the car and mum fell in as required.

All was fine until we got close to home when she began to get concerned. Where we were wasn't where she thought she lived. She was looking for a flat and we were going to a terraced house. I was fast becoming the villain and trying to take her somewhere she didn't want to go. After much reassurance and shunting her in the right direction, we got in the front door. She was puffing with exhaustion from such a long walk and panic, but her world started to become familiar again. It took about fifteen minutes for her memory to turn full cycle until she didn't remember where she had been, even that she had been out anywhere, and so was becoming settled again.

The chair would be delivered seven to fourteen days, when we would have to remove the faithful old sofa, now a mottled array of stains and all but two inches off the floor, confirmation of my compression theory. Her surroundings will change just a little. Therein lies another exciting adventchair!
Love Greg

This event was one of the many small interactions that made it clear to me that dementia had now been added to the list of problems. Fifteen minutes, I gauged was roughly the memory turn round.

That poses an important question. How does that work with schizophrenia? If you don't have continuous memory, can you still suffer from that condition? What part of your memory is affected, and how does that effect your behaviour? These are questions I would still like to know the answers to, but actually, for us at this point it really doesn't matter. Again, it is who we were managing. The causes had long become almost irrelevant.

The chair story gives an insight as to how her behaviour was at that time, and state of mind. The flat she was looking for was one she lived in and was bombed out of in war time in East London.

It was soon after this I had again taken her out in my car. When we got home, she wouldn't get out of the car. I was just starting a new relationship and was due to meet on a date that evening. A hard one to explain. As a grown adult, I might have to say, 'Sorry I'm late but my mother wouldn't get out of my car.' I was getting very frustrated, but she wasn't moving. I called my sister, who found it very amusing, but still, she wouldn't move. Neighbours would walk past from the close she lived in. They all knew who she was, some better than others. Each would have a go and try persuading her, but she wouldn't move. It didn't matter how irritated I got, the shutters were down, and nothing was going to change her mind, until she was ready to move. And who knew what was required to make that happen. This determination had been behind her behaviour for many decades. It makes me wonder if she would've survived without it. Would she have coped better? Maybe it kept her alive. You will see how perhaps it did as events progress further.

CHAPTER 27

FATHER DIED

My father had lived on his own in his house reasonably independently till he was ninety. The last year of his life was hard, and in all honesty was one year too long. We had tried to make his home as suitable as we could, and in that last year one of us would go and have lunch with him every day. I once made him bangers and mash, making a smiley face with the bangers and green pea hair. It made him smile. But he was beginning to try to cut the table rather than the food on his plate. He was just wearing out.

I have the picture in my mind of him climbing the stairs in his dressing gown, the belt hanging down in front of his feet waiting for him to trip up. He never did. He had carers going in to help him once he eventually conceded he needed some help, but after his ninety-first birthday in November, he was running down.

It has become a family tradition, twice a year for the children, brother and sister, niece and nephew to come to my house on first the Saturday at the end of April, and secondly the Saturday just before Christmas for lunch. It was a tradition started when I was fifteen by my brother, who came home one Saturday and cooked a foreign dish as it was at home then – Spaghetti Bolognese. We're talking very early seventies at this time. I decided to cook it on a regular basis, firstly just at home for whoever was around for Saturday lunch, and then subsequently developing into two Saturdays a year as mentioned. And so, the story continues. There have been a few years when life has got in the way, but mostly this has been happening now for over half a century! The April date was both my birthday and my sister-in-law's birthday and within a few weeks also my daughter and now my niece's son, so served first as a double, treble and now quadruple celebration.

My dad was always fond of his food, and the spaghetti I cooked was one of his favourites. The main dish is followed by an ever-growing cheeseboard, which has now almost taken over front stage of the meal. Since he died, we have held it as an early evening event instead for the change, and also to make it easier to allow everyone to attend, as partners were growing the numbers, and they would have to try and make it work with their families too.

Christmas 2011, Dad was having difficulty walking, so my brother picked him up and I acquired a wheelchair to make it easy for him to get into the house from the car. He 'woofed' down his lunch as he would say and appeared to enjoy himself although not very conversational. My brother dropped him home safety later that day, but that evening he collapsed in the hall where it seems he spent most of the night. He spent the next few weeks in hospital where he died peacefully whilst being well cared for. He was ninety-one.

CHAPTER 28

CARE

My mother always thought she still saw my dad frequently, when in fact she hadn't seen him for a while. So, we took the decision not to tell her he had passed away. It would serve no purpose as she was unlikely to take it in. Whereas she was happy, even though she wasn't seeing him anyway, to believe her husband still visited.

Just a few months later, we were up for another contest with social services. It had become clear that the carers who helped my mum were being stretched, and with her being only just mobile, quite heavy to manoeuvre and doubly incontinent that she needed more care. There were technical issues about funding, but we had a medical professional come in to assess. We were all there, and in true timely fashion, my mother had what one could only call an 'explosion'. My brother and I left the house leaving the two ladies to cope with the aftermath.

Not everybody was in favour of my mother going into a home, but now at ninety-one, it was clearly becoming a necessity. It was the only way she could be properly and safely cared for.

My sister and I visited several care homes locally, and settled on one we were happy with which, coincidentally, and luckily, was only a walk around the corner. We knew this was going to be a monumental task. We liaised with the home when she would be coming and made any arrangements we needed.

Task was. How did we do it.

We could not prepare her. Any fore warning would have made the mission impossible. Whatever her reason might've been, we all knew she was not going to want to do anything we had arranged, however necessary. There was no easy way.

We had a wheelchair from the home to wheel her around in. First objective. To get her in it. My mum always liked cakes and cream. We even put one on the seat of the wheelchair to get her to move over onto it, but she grabbed it and demolished it.

It took us a good few hours, a lot of stress and strain to eventually persuade her into the wheelchair, but that wasn't going to be the end of it. Now realising we were taking her somewhere, she wasn't going to let us move her easily. At the door, the picture was like that cartoon character. Two straight legs and arms on the door frame. Desperately trying not to go through. Even though we knew she didn't really know anything about what was going on, it was such a hard thing to do. The action, the emotion, the upset of having to force your mum to do something, physically she was determined not to do. To try and persuade her to pull in her arms and legs one by one whilst trying to get that chair through the front door, her aggressively resisting, upset and distraught. After a while, with not much room to manoeuvre, we turned the chair round and whisked her through backwards before she could think any more about it.

CHAPTER 29

CARE HOME

We did it and pushed her down the path. Within minutes she was calm and accepting. I certainly was not. I have no doubt it was traumatic for her at that moment, but it seemed to pass so quickly for her. There seemed to be an acceptance as the idea passed through her mind. But for the rest of us getting her into the home was the next hurdle.

It was less than ten minutes down the road till we were at the home where we were greeted by one of the staff. We wheeled her through the front door and into one of the reception rooms where they offered her some tea or orange, I think. The one she wanted they didn't offer at first. But she asked. I guess you might call that assertive given we had just forced her out of her home. She already seemed to be responding to the care and attention, just as she did in the psychiatric hospital when she was sectioned. We soon retreated once it was clear she was settling and ok.

In a way as we had seen before, Mum contradictorily had a slightly naïve trust in a childish way. When she was amongst people who she sensed were there to look after her, she gave herself up easily to it, as a child does perhaps to a parent, or a believer to their religion. There was an innocent trust that she would be looked after, and she could take that as given. She had a vulnerable and accepting side, which contrasted so strongly to the fight she had put up at least most of her adult life.

She settled well into the home, which I have to say did the best job of looking after and caring for her. Company was clearly a good thing, whether she engaged with it or not. She had been known at first to swing her ninety-one year old fists at the staff trying to hoist her and apply personal hygiene as she was now deemed as immobile, but everyone needs a little time to adapt, trust and get used to a new environment of care especially when you don't really understand where it is coming from

She was one of the eldest in the home.

My brother, sister and I had spent the last few months meeting up and clearing what was the family home in which my dad lived. Due to some medical circumstances, mornings were difficult, so we would meet early afternoon. My sister would usually bring the cream cakes for afternoon tea, and we would spend a few hours sifting through the layers of history dad had put down for those 'just in case' moments.

As expected, and true to this story, we all had our different ways of coping and dealing with this arduous and challenging chore. One would want to work through everything, sort it all and recycle as much as possible. Another would open everything, read instructions, ponder, and not want to throw much away, whilst the last wanted to sort quickly and get the job done and dusted. We soon realised we had to agree a rule between us that if there was something any one person wanted, and we were all happy, it had to be taken away that day. That didn't stop two cars being filled up, not to be emptied for a while in one case, but the rule meant we could eventually get everything cleared. In the end, when we all had satisfied ourselves and more importantly felt we had some closure, I booked a truck to come and take any remaining rubbish to finally clear the house for selling.

Thankfully clearing my mum's house was a simpler process. Not being the family home meant the ties weren't the same, and the stock not so great! It wasn't to be sold but rented as the fees for care homes are astronomical, and funds were inevitably needed to help cover costs. I remember clearing the drinks cupboard, in which I think were some bottles mum may have taken to Milton Keynes many years before. One in particular, a bottle of ruby port. The ruby, now very tired, had decided to rest in the bottom of the bottle, whilst the remainder of the port was clear to the cork! Well mum was never a party girl or a drinker. She might've had a small sherry once or twice in her younger days I'm told. In more recent years when she was in Sutton, I took her to a pub because she fancied a half of Guinness. A hangover I think from the days when pregnant mothers were encouraged to have one for health reasons.

Mum's house was a state. It needed a complete clean and redecoration, new kitchen and boiler. Her ability to keep the house clean, or even have an awareness of its cleanliness through those more recent troubled times meant it was an impossible task for her. She needed care to be able to survive. Carers coming in several time a day just weren't enough anymore. She needed looking after and was in the right place.

CHAPTER 30

HOSPITAL SEPSIS

After a few years in the home, we were informed mum had been taken into hospital. A surprise as nothing had been flagged. In A&E she was diagnosed as having sepsis. Not something to be taken lightly, and often has a bad ending, particularly when you're in your mid-nineties.

The A&E doctor told us he wasn't sure which way it was going to go. He was pumping antibiotics into her intravenously. He would know in under an hour if she would get through. My sister sat with her, and I remember her describing my mum's reaction at one point as if something terrible was happening to her, a shudder with fear on her face as if her body was in a mighty clash. Which of course it was. It was being poisoned. But extraordinarily within a few hours it was clear she was going to be ok. In fact, by next morning, she was right as rain and chatty.

Now, there were a few times my mum was in hospital. The second was when we had found her sitting apparently asleep, in her chair at home showing no reaction to anything we did. We couldn't wake her up, but she was breathing. She didn't respond to calls, nudges prods or pulls, anything at all. Obviously being worried we called for an ambulance. The paramedic arrived, conducted a few tests, which apparently seemed to show nothing serious. He then conducted a very highly skilled technical procedure, which was to prove pivotal. He pinched her very hard between her thumb and forefinger. After what must have been an hour or more comatose, she jumped into life instantly and was immediately looking around for the perpetrator. Once she registered we were all around she was a little confused, but fine. She was taken into hospital for a check-up, but she decided she'd like to stay a while. For whatever reason, she had decided she wanted to stay where she was. Several people with varying status were trying to get her into an ambulance and home, but she wasn't having it. There was no obvious reason. It was a bit like getting her out of my car that time, except she was in hospital and there much longer than necessary. She couldn't be physically forced, even less reasoned with. She just didn't want to move. But eventually to the relief of all the staff, she decided it was time to go.

CHAPTER 31

PASSING

Mum settled back into the home and seemed content. I visited her quite frequently, though the thought she was cared for and others, professionals, were fundamentally taking responsibility for her care was still such a relief to us all. When she first went in, we all took a step back and sighed a huge sigh of relief. The need for that constant concern and worry that anything might happen had been taken off our hands when she was ninety-one years old.

For every 5 people with schizophrenia:

- *1 will get better within 5 years of their first obvious symptoms.*
- *3 will get better but will have times when they get worse again.*
- *1 will have troublesome symptoms for long periods of time.*

- Rethink Mental Illness

Mum was the one in five to have troublesome periods, for most of the rest of her time. But her personality was changed by her troubles. Life would change over the years, but it was a gradual lurch from one problem to another. And for most of those years she could never be a wife to her husband, a mother to her children, a grandmother to her grandchildren or even a friend to anybody. That was a loss for all of us and all the consequent ramifications. But it was also a tragic loss for her. Like us, neither would she benefit from the loving relationships, warmth, hugs and cuddles there to be had from big people and little ones alike. Those things that aren't just a treat at the time but warm you to your very bones. Still the world would carry on around her.

She would sit amongst the other ever-changing residents, who didn't seem to matter to her most of the time. She would look into my eyes, when I visited, as if she might know me, chat without any real personal connection about not very much, though I was never sure if she did know who I was. There felt like a trust, but as I said before, she seemed to have a way of accepting with expectation a safe environment. I wouldn't stay very long. There seemed no point. Little and often felt the best for us both to get the most out of my visiting. The amount of time I felt didn't make any difference but visiting more frequently instead meant a new event for her each time. As I left, I would always wave till I was out of sight. I'd try and read how she was reacting to me leaving. No sooner had I walked away her mind was somewhere else. I could stand at the door, but it appeared I had already left. Who knows what was actually going on in her mind? She had managed to find some peace there, security, though it was still clear she was always working in a parallel world. Maybe in a caring community it didn't need to be so destructive to her, and those around her. Maybe that caring community was allowing her to sit back from the turmoil life once gave her.

Either way, her fight to survive kept her going a few more years yet, relatively content and at last now without further drama.

She picked up an infection, which took hold of her now weak body and within a few days passed away peacefully in her sleep.

She was the oldest person in the home and still the only one on no medication.

She was ninety-seven.

Amen.

CHAPTER 32

AT PEACE

The infection taking a few days to get hold gave time for the priest to visit her before she passed, so fulfilling her religious beliefs which I feel sure were still rooted there. If I ever had a wish for her, and I profoundly did, it was that after a life of isolation, she didn't pass alone. That somebody was there or nearby watching and caring for her. That prayer I felt had been answered.

When I look back over this story, the story of my mum in my time, there is one thing that seems consistent throughout her life regardless of her mental state. She was always looking for somewhere she could be safe and secure, and loved too. She was close to her mum, but her dad was challenging. She was married, but in time the marriage didn't seem to look after her needs enough, as they were changing. She became isolated, isolating herself, eventually trying to be self-sufficient. Protecting herself maybe. Maybe even protecting others. I can't help thinking she felt lost while she tried to work out her path of coping with life as her head allowed. And yet, as time eventually passed in her life, she gave up to carers, to the hospital who would look after her, the home she went into, which would care and keep her secure. For her, safe environments. It was as if she had a fundamental, even naive trust in the institutions of our society. And so ironically in the end, 'only if she gave her consent' meaning that she had given up to it. That she had the capacity to give way. Not something she had always been able to do voluntarily.

Thankfully they all eventually met her needs and gave her a settled and secure contentment, so allowing her a more peaceful life mostly, for her last six years.

Of course, there was so much that complicated every step of her life and how she could or couldn't manage it. The effects of her mental illness and consequences that made life impossible for decades. I mentioned earlier the three saddest moments I remember in my life. The first being when my mum came out of hospital, and I realised she could never be normal. The second is unconnected to this story but nevertheless one of the hardest moments of having to tell my three children that their mother and I were separating. And the third is one that, again hit me unexpectedly and yet was obvious.

My brother, sister and I were visiting the priest to organise the funeral for my mother. We talked through a few of the necessary details and then the priest turned to us and asked, 'When I speak about your mother at the funeral, what can you tell me about her? Who was she? What were her interests, hobbies, things she liked to do, and things she perhaps achieved?'

We sat in silence for a moment.

My sister mentioned she was an avid reader, which was once true. But I had no memory of it.

It dawned on me that not one of us could think of one thing. No interests. No hobbies. No friends or activities. Nothing.

She had been consumed by her mental state, and all that meant for her. That was such a tragedy for her and her life.

Perhaps her garden in Milton Keynes?

But that became more of a solitary and necessary therapy than a hobby or interest. An occupation for her soon lost when she moved back to Sutton. Perhaps we could say travelling. Though a desire she long had and one she technically achieved in her late fifties, I'm not sure I could list it as an experience in the way normal people love traveling.

But it also consolidated the fact in my mind that if I didn't know what her life would've been like had she had the freedom to live it, then I didn't know her as a person. I didn't know who she really was. She didn't want to be ill. It wasn't her fault. By her way of trying to manage I did feel . . . know . . . she was a good person and she was my mum. But who could she have been?

I always felt I knew her. But what would she have really been like if we had been able to have a good relationship? Played together, a game, hugged, messed around or just conversation? Went places together, had fun. What would she think about . . . well anything? People, events, food, travel and places. What would she say if she had come to my school, if she sat down to help or support me, give me advice? Dealt with me in those frustrating days as a teenager! I had a connection with her because she was my mum, but I didn't know 'who' she was.

CHAPTER 33

CONSEQUENCE

It struck me as I was writing those last paragraphs, that although my work was trying to cover the story of my mum, her mental health and how I dealt with it, there was another aspect which was inevitably pivotal.

The other parent.

My dad was known as a kind and polite gentleman with a heart of gold, as a fundamental of who he was. He worked hard and provided us with a stability and a secure financial life. As he progressed, we went from being a family very careful with money to more comfortable as the family grew. From working class to the middle classes, if you will. In truth with the circumstances, there was little money spent on holidays in the early days, none on days out or entertainment, or extravagances. Mum didn't drive, and my dad had a company car. Eventually we owned our own house. We were ok.

One would expect trying to hold down both a good job and managing home life was a challenge, and not one my dad found he could do easily. There were company dos, which he couldn't take his wife to. As a rising employee in the company this was not something in those days that was easily explained or even perhaps well received. He had little or no partner support. Then, as in many businesses, end of month was a busy and pressured time for him, and support at home wasn't always there. In earlier years, I'm sure there were attempts to be supportive, but as my mother's problems intensified, minds separated.

My dad often used to whistle a tune, or sing a song, but was renowned for never knowing the words. He had a jolly disposition, but you would do well if you could get him to answer a question. He very rarely lost his temper, and when mum had complained to him about me, he just would say to me - try not to argue. There were many times, especially in my teenage years, when my dad took the full force of mum constantly 'having a go at him'. Not many would have stood up to that without blowing a gasket or be affected by the constant barrage. And it would be wrong not to consider the consequences on my dad's own adult development.

Maybe he would've learnt those words, danced more, bought more records for that radiogram and partied just a little bit. I think he would. Let alone any other interests that may have evolved. And by being able to do all those things and perhaps more, he might've become more of that role model that I was desperately needing. The predicament was difficult, but for me his passive approach was frustratingly evasive.

It became clear in my early twenties that dad had a companion he spent some time with. I would drive to the West End in the evenings to work as a showman in the West End Theatre, passing him the other way driving out of London with a lady sat next to him. He wouldn't get home till late most evenings. It was his way of surviving the situation I suppose but my point of including this is the part he therefore played at home for me.

He genuinely worked long hours some of the time, but not at others. This gave my dad a secret, and holding a secret meant he could not be open and properly himself at home.

If he had had the choice to be happily married with his family, of course that would've been his wish. But everybody was surviving. He admirably stood by my mum in terms of looking after her financially and for her security. He facilitated her move to Milton Keynes, though felt in a way she was breaking their relationship and leaving him and didn't think she should go. He visited her frequently, once a week, when she was local, to help and sort out any finances, and she trusted him always to look after her. He also often travelled to Milton Keynes to visit her, something he perhaps didn't need to do. And as I said, even after he died, still in her mind she thought he visited her every week.

But what did his roll mean for me amongst the turmoil of home.

He didn't really play an active role.

Certainly, in my teenage years he was absent, but there. I spent less time with him than my mum inevitably, but his time was shared, and he always had that secret. As I have described, visits to parent teacher meetings were often late or absent. He fell asleep in my school production. When you have a secret, you can't have an open conversation with your children. When deciding what to do when I left school, I don't remember any help or support. I had a role model, but he wasn't an active one.

Over the years, I often would drop in on my dad for a cup of tea. Something I would always enjoy. My brother, sister and I would call him The Drums. He would talk to us all at different times and pick up the gossip before we could talk to each other, if we did. Communication between siblings is often variable, especially as we were eight years apart top to bottom.

In his later years, when I dropped in, he would reminisce a lot. He would enjoy returning to the East End, where his roots were for funerals and long chats to talk about the old times, and what had changed. Do you remember so and so? I took him a few times.

But when he would reminisce at home it would always be about that life in the East End. It would never be about his own family life. At first, I used to wait and listen for a recollection about our family, and because it never came, I would feel somehow it didn't exist. It had been cancelled.

I assumed there was nothing he had or wished to remember.

So, for me, I knew him a little, but again we had few family activities, events, days out, family times and good family relationships. When I thought back over my life, I realised I didn't really know him either.

There was little or no real active interest from him. No real encouragement.

Because he wasn't really there.

There was no interest from mum.

Because she wasn't really there.

If I were to sit back and think about what traits or talents I might have inherited from my parents. How would I know?

He didn't offer hugs, or any physical contact after I was quite young, and from my memory there he was often tired. The hugs only came about again in his later years. Not instigated by him, but by us in his declining years. Of course, he was a good-hearted man and managed as best he could, but he was frozen out of ways to express his feelings or be involved. For me that meant he was distant.

He too was a victim of these far reaching consequences as much as everybody else, demonstrating how mental illness affects the whole family environment.

CHAPTER 34

THE BIGGER PICTURE

When dad died, we had, as always, the conversation about where his ashes should lie. And again, true to our history, we each had a different view. One of them was to eventually put his ashes in with mum, when she finally passed. She wished to be buried, but we never expected that to be another six years.

And so, as with the time when we got together to clear dad's house with our very different approaches, again we all started with strong feelings. But after a period, when the 'ashes' had settled so to speak, it all became less important. As life moved on and we stepped back with more perspective, the events and time took over my initial reactions and where his ashes were to lay was less of an issue for me, and I was happy for them to lay at peace wherever. That was to be with my mum, in her coffin, with her.

Consequently, as I eventually sit back and looked at the big picture surrounding my writing, there are two directions to which my thoughts travel.

The first is the love story of my mum and dad that shines out from behind those dark clouds. Though that part of the story is, at first, hard to pick out because it becomes wrapped up in so much adversity, in essence this was from where everything evolved. From their school days together to their happy courting days, their early days of adulthood and marriage, they were a team. Taking the big step to move from the East End and making a new, better life in Surrey for themselves and their family. There were surely storms, tornados and blizzards along the way, but dad looked after mum for seventy years of their marriage as best he could. They were never divorced. And for her last six years, he was always in her heart. She always carried him with her and believed he still regularly visited and looked after her.

The second direction is that of a woman who had she not had that difficult start in life but could have taken advantage of opportunities and care available, may have survived to achieve so much. Even with the challenges of her circumstances and mental health, she still came back from a tormented existence to travelling up to Harley Street getting her teeth fixed and making herself presentable again, trying to engage with life once more. She took her independence to move to Milton Keynes, living on her own for several years. Organised herself to go traveling to Hong Kong and Australia. And if she could've really lived that life of freedom, how different her husband and family's lives may have been, her children and her grandchildren too.

She was to believe that none of this was available to her, but if she could've known what might've been, if she had been dealt a different hand, if she'd had that chance . . .

> Until I started to write this book,
> I didn't think I had a story to tell.

AFTERWORD

Although, of course, all my immediate family play a part in this story, I can only write this as 'my story', how my mother's mental health affected her life as I saw it as well as mine, and consequently how as a family we managed events.

I haven't necessarily mentioned everything we each did to keep things going. As one would expect my father, brother, sister, and myself all played our parts in getting through. We each played our part when we could and as well as we could give each of our own situations, different ages, our own lives and where we were with each of our families and relationships.

That meant circumstances were very different for each of us at any given moment. When times required, we communicated and decided a course of direction and worked together as best we could, each with their own strengths to suite that given moment. We worked together and managed difficult situations every time they came up, and I feel proud that we all managed to do that. We all survived in our own ways, and I strongly believe that was an achievement in itself. Here, I can only speak for myself and my experience.

As I realised when I discovered the National Schizophrenic Fellowship how important it is to be able to identify issues you are dealing with, understanding and consequently support if available means so much in a journey. Hopefully also trying to share some of my feelings and experiences may strike a chord with some on their own journey.

For family members of people with schizophrenia:
It can be hard to understand what is happening if your son or daughter, husband or wife, brother or sister develops schizophrenia. Sometimes, no-one realises what is wrong.
Royal College of Psychiatrists

It is interesting to note that when referring to the Royal College of Psychiatrists website under 'family members of people with schizophrenia' it refers to siblings, partners and children. The assumption is, I suppose that there is always an adult in the room to manage the predicament. But when the parent is the sufferer, who is looking out for those children affected. Yes, my dad was a partner, but there were also children, and as is also said above, *'It can be hard to understand what is happening'*. That means for everybody including adults. Who is caring and supporting, loving and helping them to understand what is going on. After all, *'Sometimes no-one realises what is wrong'*. Filling in all those gaps which are inevitably there that aren't even realised. Helping to realise this isn't normal and they are ok.

Who is looking out for those children?

When talking to an addict, an addict of any type, they will tell you that nobody understands that feeling they have when temptation is upon them, their need to do something, whether it be placing that bet, taking that drink, drugs or any other addiction. If an addict can connect with a group of like-minded people, people sharing that addiction, they know they are in a place where those people understand what they are going through, what their thoughts and feelings are when they are at that critical point of irresistible temptation and are in trouble. Only someone in that same situation can truly understand it. My mum couldn't have that. She was alone in her troubles. But some others and carers can.

I am not suggesting addiction is the same as the mental illness I have talked about in this story, but to those dealing with mental health issues, whether suffering or caring, the benefit of connecting with people who have like experience in a world where you feel very alone cannot only be a life saver, but gives you hope to be able to tackle everything it throws in your path.

But for the child, the danger of coping with such illnesses is they take a space in your mind, there is an imprint. As a child growing up that space is instinctively made and doesn't necessarily go away. And so however that illness you are managing develops or changes, there is always that space in your mind to try to cope with it. As life moves on that space may always be filled, not necessarily with the initial emotional trauma, but with any other situation with another who may be close to you. The initial preoccupation of managing your life with a parent and mental illness forces you give priority to it and as a weight can stem ability to develop. If the initial problem subsides or goes away there is a tendency to instead of feeling free, to fill that space with another problem, consequently stifling the ability to move forward. Something else will always fill that void making normality hard to achieve.

When I read the introduction for Anna Wilson's book at the Dartington 'Ways with Words' Festival and immediately wanted to ask how she felt it had affected her life, I knew there would be many people who would have questions to ask.

Anna is of course an experienced, talented professional writer and I suspect her most important skill and ability within her book will be to tell her story and particularly to connect with those who have had comparable experiences, and for that alone I'm sure her book will be very valuable.

Perhaps now is the time for me to read it.

I haven't forgotten you Tigger.

ACKNOWLEDGMENTS

The process of writing this story caused me to look for other peoples' written experiences, which might be comparable to mine. I began with a book *The snipers we couldn't see* by Karen Comba. At first, I was disappointed that her mother, who was suffering mental illness, was already having treatment, albeit crude of its day, and Karen also suffered physical abuse. I thought our stories were too different. But I persisted and I found the same language and feeling in her story. I wrote to her and received back the most wonderful empathetic and supportive letter. Many circumstances and geography may have been different but mental illness is universal, its consequences felt are the same for sufferers and family. Just finding those connections felt so valuable to me. Karen now does much valuable supportive work in the States including hosting a TV programme.

    I then came across the well-known political journalist Isobel Hardman's book *The Natural Health*

Service, which amongst many things so clearly spelled out how we can understand our own mental health and manage it in the best way possible. I feel sure my mum's gardening project was a natural way for her to survive and find some comfort.

Christina Patterson, an established journalist wrote her family memoir *Outside the Sky is Blue*, which again I first thought was very different to my story, but it also became clear there were many common elements.

Surviving Schizophrenia was written by Louise Gillett, a brilliant story of her own success in surviving the illness and demonstrating a different and brave perspective not many would be able to convey.

And finally having watched David Harewood's story on the BBC relating his experience and desire to understand the psychosis he suffered from in his twenties, I found myself communicating with Dr David Jones from the Open University. A senior lecturer in Psychology, he wrote a book *Myths Madness and the Family*. The Impact of Mental Illness on the family. In particular this gave me the real perspective on grief which I had already naturally conveyed within my story, but without quite understanding it was 'grief' I was experiencing.

None of these books I read during my writing were what I was initially looking for. I was trying to find someone with the same circumstances as me. A young boy growing up with a mother suffering from undiagnosed schizophrenia. As yet I have not been able to find that story elsewhere.

I must thank Gary Smailes at Bubblecow for helping me in editing this story. I could not effectively separate myself enough to be objective, and so his skills were invaluable.

My thanks to Rethink Mental Illness, Living with Schizophrenia and The Royal College of Psychiatrists for some of those vital facts needed to demonstrate what it can be like 'as life goes on'

I also have to thank my friends who read my story and shared their thoughts. All were invaluable and helped me to see and give me a broader vision.

On my journey I have however discovered a valuable charity called *Our Time* who's aim is to support children of parents with mental illness. Had that have been available for me I would have had a foot on the ground, an understanding in real time and a shared support. So if you have read this and it has also been your story, I hope sharing offers you some solace and satisfaction that others know and understand what you too have been through.

For me the writing in itself has been amazing.

For me this has been the best way to tell this story to my now grown up children.

For me if sharing has helped anybody in any way, that is enough.

Printed in Great Britain
by Amazon